THE 7 MINUTE SEX SECRET

Martica K Heaner, originally from Texas, has lived in London for several years. She was awarded UK 1992 Fitness Leader of the Year and nominated for an award for Special Achievement in the Fitness Industry in 1994. She was a British Aerobics Champion Silver Medallist in 1989 and is certified by ACE and AFAA. She writes regularly for many leading magazines and newspapers and is the author of *Curves – The Body Transformation Strategy*. She is also featured on the bestselling video, 'Thighs, Tums and Bums'.

Also by Martica K Heaner

Curves: The Body Transformation Strategy
How to Be a Personal Trainer
Secrets of an Aerobics Instructor

The 7 Minute Sex Secret

Martica K Heaner

CORONET BOOKS
Hodder and Stoughton

First published in Great Britain in 1995
by Hodder & Stoughton
A division of Hodder Headline PLC
A Coronet paperback

10 9 8 7 6 5 4 3 2 1

British Library Cataloguing in Publication Data

Heaner, Martica K.
7 Minute Sex Secret
I. Title
613.954

ISBN 0 340 62860 X

Typeset by Palimpsest Book Production Limited,
Polmont, Stirlingshire
Printed and bound in Great Britain by
Cox & Wyman Ltd, Reading, Berkshire

Hodder and Stoughton
A division of Hodder Headline PLC
338 Euston Road
London NW1 3BH

CONTENTS

ACKNOWLEDGEMENTS

Special thanks to William H Masters MD of the Masters & Johnson Institute in St Louis for taking the time to answer my questions.

Thank you

Dr Stephen Lincoln.

My friends Stephen Saltzman and Tamara Chant for dinner parties over the years which have been an endless source of inspiration!

My agent, Darley Anderson and my editor, Rowena Webb at Hodder & Stoughton, for believing I was old enough to write this book!

Wayne Westcott PhD, Fitness/Research Director at the South Shore YMCA, Massachussetts; Kate Roylance, Head of Physiotherapy at the Portland Women's Hospital, London; Dr John Osborne MD, Prof Ob/Gyn at University College, University of London; the British Medical Association.

John Lasser MS, PhD pending in Psychology at the University of Texas, Austin; Mrs Kernoghan at Colgate Medical.

CHAPTER ONE

Fit for Pleasure

Forget all the how-to manuals which show you new positions. Forget all the guides which lead you step-by-step from blow job to cunnilingus. Forget trying to memorize how to do *what* where and for how long. There's a simple exercise you can do which can dramatically improve the frequency and intensity of your orgasms. If your sex life is already good, it can be better. And if you've never had an orgasm, or have difficulty with them during intercourse because you don't receive enough stimulation, these exercises can increase the sensations of pleasure. The secret is a method advocated by gynaecologists, sex therapists and erotic dancers worldwide which has been refined to make it even more effective. The simple moves I will show you not only improve sex, they improve your health by combatting the physical effects of ageing, rectify the effects of childbirth and lower your risk of future genital dysfunction.

SEXUAL SUCCESS

Sex is a lot of things. It's an expression of love, a life-creating act. It's an emotional and spiritual bond. It's guttural passion, animal lust, play between adults. Sex, for some Eastern traditions, is the harmony of energy which brings the lovers to a higher consciousness. No one will deny that sex is the most natural act that exists. To ensure that we do it, both male and females have specific sex organs whose sole function is to give pleasure. Pleasure that, at its best, is so enticing, so exhilarating, *so orgasmic*, it makes you want to have sex over and over again. But the amount of pleasure each of us derives from sex varies immensely, especially among women.

Most men are guaranteed an orgasm every time they have sex, providing everything is in working order. Women aren't so predictable. Some women experience one or even multiple climaxes each time they make love. But others are lucky if they come close. And more than just a few women have quite a frustrating time of it. Several surveys, including The Janus Report on Sexual Behaviour, have shown that almost 10 to 20 per cent of women in America never have orgasms. The *Hite Report on Sexuality* reveals that even if they are capable of it, 70 per cent cannot have an orgasm from intercourse alone. Several informal woman's magazine surveys in the UK show similar results.

All in all, the inability to achieve orgasm through lovemaking can be a bit of a let-down, because it has become more and more the case in the West that the enjoyment of sex is largely measured by the number and intensity of orgasms experienced. Those who are frank about their sexual experiences might make comments like, 'I had the most incredible climax last night', or 'He was amazing – we did it three times!'. Oh sure, we all love the intimacy of just being close to our lover and any feelings of arousal are undoubtedly enjoyable. But as these comments show, it's the final build-up and explosion of sexual tension which usually determines the quality of the experience.

SEXUAL EROGENOUS ZONES

Books on the subject proliferate. Many examine the multitude of possible positions lovers can jiggle and wriggle their way into. Others espouse various techniques to enhance foreplay; they identify ways of licking, touching, sucking and nibbling various erogenous zones all over the body. Still others get scientific by identifying sensitive areas which lead to climax. The most famous is the G-spot, discovered by German gynaecologist, Ernest Gräfenberg. This is an area of tissue on the innermost side of the vagina, closely related in composition to the male prostate. Stimulation here is said to elicit a vaginal, rather than clitoral orgasm which is often accompanied by female ejaculation. While there are definitely a wide range of orgasmic responses, some of which are felt more deeply than others, most sexologists agree that all orgasms are ultimately linked to the clitoris, either directly or indirectly.

Other researchers have identified a pleasure area around the entrance to the urethra, the U-spot, which is evidently connected to the G-spot. And most recently, one gynaecologist has coined the term S-zone for the area around the entrance to the vagina which has a pleasurable response to being stretched. The problem is, all of these spots appear to be very subjective. Even the researchers are in disagreement over their actual existence. Under laboratory testing, some women apparently experience sensations from these areas, while others simply do not.

Everyone is so busy looking for new spots that they forget we already have a very powerful one, the C-spot, or the clitoris. Unlike the others, it's existence is not in question, it's not hard to find and it generally works, it's just a matter of stimulating it in the right way. While there are definitely a wide range of orgasmic responses, some which are felt more deeply than others, most sexologists agree that all orgasms are ultimately linked to the clitoris, either directly or indirectly.

SEXUAL AROUSAL

An orgasm is the pleasurable release, or sometimes, *explosion*, of built-up sexual tension. But experiencing orgasms is not as simple as touching the C-spot and boom, you climax. Your body has a specific arousal pattern which must take place for the desired end-result to occur. And while there are a multitude of reasons why the pattern can be interrupted, there are exercises which can set up the physiological scenario to help keep you on track.

In the Sixties, famed sex researchers William Masters MD and Virginia Johnson identified the physiological reactions to arousal. They divided the whole process of human sexual response into four stages: excitement, plateau, orgasmic, and resolution. The amount of time spent in each phase can vary, but ultimately, for orgasm to occur there needs to be enough stimulation to progress to each stage. It appears that women who have never or rarely have orgasms, may be stuck in the excitement or plateau phase. It may be because a partner orgasms too soon and stops so there is insufficient stimulation for her to enter the next phase. Or there may not be enough sexual tension from clitoral stimulation during love-making for her to do so. But research has shown that all healthy women are capable of progressing to the next phases. They just need the appropriate stimulus.

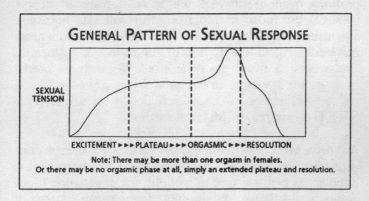

GENERAL PATTERN OF SEXUAL RESPONSE

SEXUAL
TENSION

EXCITEMENT ▶ ▶ ▶ PLATEAU ▶ ▶ ▶ ORGASMIC ▶ ▶ ▶ RESOLUTION

Note: There may be more than one orgasm in females.
Or there may be no orgasmic phase at all, simply an extended plateau and resolution.

Many women simply need to learn where and how to touch in order to build up enough sexual tension to orgasm. Several studies have shown that women who masturbate find it easier to achieve an orgasm during sex. But even when women are able to masturbate successfully, when it comes down to sex with a partner they may still have difficulties. During oral and manual sex obviously the skill of their partner is important; however, during intercourse many women simply do not get enough direct stimulation of the C-spot to come. There are a few positions where you or your partner can manually stimulate the clitoris, but in the most common ones – you or him on top – it's physically impossible to squeeze a hand in between two crushed bodies and still maintain control, balance and the necessary rhythm. You can manipulate yourself into a variety of positions, but the fact is, very few of them provide direct contact with a woman's C-spot.

Not widely recognized is the fact that it's possible to have an orgasm from *indirect* stimulation to the C-spot. In fact, there is research which shows that simple exercises to condition the vaginal muscles may be all that many women need to provide the extra stimulation to the clitoris. Enhanced muscular control will also help you to manoeuvre your pelvis at subtle angles to attain a more pleasurable position. If it is in good functioning health, the vagina is more easily aroused. While most of the popular sex books have explored seemingly every detail of copulation, none of them have deeply investigated the effects of vaginal health on pleasure.

To be fair, sex research is relatively new. Masters and Johnson were among the first to explore the physiological states of sex, and while there has been a vast amount of medical research on the sex organs, the focus has been primarily on the treatment and prevention of diseased states, or on fertility and childbirth. Little of the accumulated knowledge has been applied directly to sexual functioning.

Of the research that exists, there is ample evidence to suggest that sexual health is key to sexual arousal. Much of the vaginal area consists of muscle. Since C-spot arousal causes this muscle to become more active, and stronger muscles mean greater sensitivity, conditioning this area can lead to better sex.

SEXERCISE

Overall health is crucial to optimum sexual functioning. You can't have great sex unless your body is fine-tuned, nourished, and well-rested. If you are out of shape, don't eat or sleep well, you may be more fatigued than aroused.

Exercise has been shown to give extraordinary erotic energy boosts; many studies have proved the positive effects particularly of endurance exercise on sex. Subjects have reported increased sexual desire and satisfaction after participating in regular exercise such as swimming, running, cycling and aerobics. One study by American physiologist Linda De Villers found 40 per cent of the 8000 women surveyed noticed an increase in their ability to become aroused after beginning a regular exercise programme. Twenty-six per cent found it easier to reach climax. Since exercise stimulates the endocrine glands, increasing testosterone, the sex hormone levels, the libido – or sex drive – is heightened.

Breathing and heart rates speed up during sex. Muscles, particularly in the hips and thighs, can be pushed to their limit from repetitive thrusting. So the improved cardio-vascular and muscular stamina you experience from regular training translates into less fatigue in the bedroom.

Furthermore conditioned muscles result in more muscle fibres with an increased number of blood vessels throughout the body. Their greater efficiency along with increased blood volume means better overall circulation. And a stronger heart and lungs mean that the blood is pumped more efficiently, using less energy to get more oxygen to the tissues. Since male and female sexual arousal is dependant upon good circulation, the increased and more efficient blood supply enhances the ability of the sex organs to become lubricated and erect.

All types of exercise improve the nerve pathways between the brain and muscles, by training the message from the brain to coordinate more efficiently through a nerve to muscle fibres. This fine-tuning makes you more receptive to and more able to focus on physical sensations. Simply put, a fitter body functions better.

Vigorous exercise is also associated with increased alpha waves in the brain. These waves are electrical patterns of brain activity which indicate that the mind is relaxed. This pleasurable state of consciousness leaves you more receptive to sex. Long duration exercise stimulates the production of brain hormones called endorphins. These block pain and promote a euphoric state. Working out leaves you in a hormonally charged 'feel-good' state. It's been proven in psychological tests that exercise contributes to increased self-esteem, decreased anxiety, and more self-confidence. The better you feel, the more receptive you'll be to sexual excitement during sex.

Of course, you can have too much of a good thing. Over-exercising (say 2–3 hours everyday) can stress the body, lowering sex drive, and even weakening the immune system.

Exercise improves all of your body functions, so, without doubt, general exercise improves your sex life. To some degree this is simply the result of overall improved health. What has never been fully explored is the effect of *specific* exercises directly related to sex. For example, while toned arms may make you look better and help protect your joints, they probably will not directly benefit your sex life. But doing exercises which are highly specific to sex can enhance sexual performance. As you will experience, exercising the love muscles – those in and around the pelvis which are actively used during sex – can most certainly make a tremendous difference.

Effects of Regular Exercise on Sex

- increased sex drive;
- enhanced ability to be aroused;
- more stamina, less fatigue;
- improved blood circulation aids erection of the clitoris and penis;
- greater receptiveness to sexual sensations;
- an increase in self-confidence.

THE LOVE MUSCLES

If you have ever had a child, you are probably familiar with the exercises done to improve the strength of the vaginal walls and pelvic floor, a sling of muscles at the base of the pelvis. A series of squeezing movements known as Kegel exercises are typically performed during pregnancy for an easier delivery, and afterwards to help the overstretched, traumatised tissues to recover.

The exercises were named after an American gynaecologist, Arnold Kegel MD, who discovered their effectiveness in the Fifties. He found that women with weak pelvic floor muscles experienced significant improvement from these moves. Not only did women recover from birth more easily, but many women who had experienced incontinence, or urine leakage, were completely cured or found their problem was alleviated. But for our purposes, the most important discovery was evidence which showed that after strengthening these muscles, women became more orgasmic and therefore enjoyed sex more than they ever had before. In some cases, women in their fifties who had never experienced an orgasm finally did and even continued doing so years later.

Kegel exercises work several different muscles in the pelvic floor. These muscles form a sort of elastic hammock underneath your pelvis, extending from the front of your pubic bone, under the vagina, all the way to the anus. They essentially hold all the organs in the lower part of your torso in their correct positions, counteracting the pulling forces of gravity. As you can imagine, when they become weak, they can sag, making everything else sink.

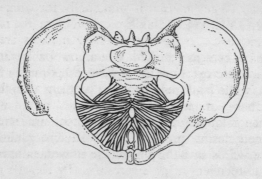

Pelvic floor muscles forming a hammock

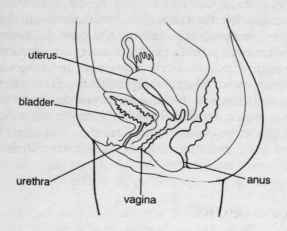

Side view of pelvic organs

So Dr Kegel developed a rudimentary way to keep them strong.

Kegel exercises are a series of repeated squeezing contractions performed usually while sitting or lying. Clinical evidence has shown that they definitely improve muscle tone and support. The standard exercise technique which Dr Kegel devised is principally for women who have already developed a physical problem like prolapse or incontinence, or for those whose muscles are being stressed by pregnancy. The effects on sex are indirect, so when these exercises are redesigned primarily for sex, as opposed to just strengthening a problem area, they can produce even more powerful results.

Gynaecologists agree that it's very important to strengthen these muscles at an early age. Different studies have shown that a surprising percentage of women have some weakness without being aware of it. Dr Kegel's clinical observations indicated that 30 to 40 per cent of women lack normal function of the perineal, or pelvic floor, muscles. This is not surprising considering that these muscles don't get as much active work as they're meant to. In the past they were used while squatting, but, today, chairs and toilets make this position largely unnecessary. Apparently tail-wagging animals rarely show impaired function of their genital muscles. It's thought that continual wagging sufficiently activates the muscles to maintain tone. Since humans lost their tails somewhere along the evolutionary line and have less cause to use these muscles in daily life, most women need to give the muscles extra exercise.

SEX AS SPORT

The pelvic floor muscles are similar to other muscles, such as the biceps in your arms, your abdominals and the quadriceps and hamstrings in the front and back of your thighs. Unlike your heart, which is an involuntary muscle (you don't consciously make it beat), the pelvic floor muscles can be voluntarily contracted. Because of this, and like the other muscles in your body, they respond to regular contractions by becoming stronger. If the stimulus is intense enough, they will also increase in size, leading to even further increases in strength; there will be an increase in overall muscle tone; and there will also be an increase in blood flow as more muscle fibre is developed.

One of the most important principles in training muscles is called specificity. That is, in order to develop specific muscular abilities, the muscles must be exercised in a way that replicates how they are to be used in a particular activity. If they are exercised in any other way, there may still be benefits, but the body won't achieve the specific training effects necessary to help you perform at your optimum level.

Simply put, to play tennis you have to train by playing tennis. But while playing tennis may make you more fit, and although you may be working out many of the same muscles, it won't make you a better dancer. You have to dance. You can't train for a marathon by swimming miles and miles, and then expect to be able to run. You may improve your stamina and endurance, but you won't develop the precise muscle coordination needed in order to run long distances. You must train by running and doing those exercises which develop muscles in the way they are used during a race.

This principle is exactly the same with Kegel exercises. You can do Kegel exercises and see improvements in the pelvic support necessary to keep you from leaking urine. The general muscle tone improvements will inadvertently help you have better sex. But since the exercises aren't designed for sex, they won't help you have *optimum* sex.

The standard pelvic floor exercises which have been practised up to now consist of doing a few repetitions of squeezing moves. As discussed, these are effective for developing the minimal amount of muscle tone necessary to rehabilitate the muscle fibres after birth, or strengthen them when a weakness already present has caused a physical dysfunction. But the muscle tone needed for *general* pelvic support is quite different, probably much less, than the muscle strength and action required during sex. So to improve sex, the Kegel exercise technique can be developed further into a series of specialised exercises specifically designed for sex.

Although this seems obvious, to date, no sex books have established more precise methods to train the pelvic floor for sex. While most mention in passing that Kegels are helpful, generally all that is advised is the standard exercise formula: locate the muscles and squeeze them between thirty and one hundred times per day. But if you want to *significantly* enhance your sex life and orgasmic ability, this standard programme is simply not enough. Basic Kegel exercises will not develop *enough* muscle strength, endurance and coordination to greatly enhance sexual performance. To do so, you need to train for sex. You must practise the exercises in such a way that they replicate the rhythms, body positions and forces present during sex.

As a fitness instructor for over thirteen years, I have taken my knowledge of fitness training and applied it to the Kegel exercises. My 7 Minute Sex Secret is a new technique which employs the latest training technology to develop sex-specific strength, endurance, coordination and agility in your vaginal muscles. Women who practise these Sex Squeezes for at least seven minutes a day can enjoy love-making in a whole new way. You can experience more powerful orgasms, or possibly even multiple orgasms. If you currently experience tenderness or a lack of sensation in your vagina which prevents you from having an orgasm, you will probably find that these exercises make sex much more enjoyable.

THE POWER OF THE MIND

Some may argue that the simple act of becoming involved with and focusing on her sex organs means a woman is more likely to orgasm compared to someone who hasn't given her pelvis a second thought in years. Indeed, there are a few women who may have strong pelvic floor muscles, but still be unable to orgasm. Sex is most definitely a very subjective experience. While there is a direct cause-and-effect relation between being stimulated and aroused, it's the psychological component which ultimately decides how enjoyable sex is. Masters and Johnson found that even when aroused, a man or woman's sexual response could immediately be stifled by other types of stimulus, whether it was a loud distracting noise, loss of mental concentration, fatigue, or emotional dissatisfaction of some kind (anxiety, anger, insecurity). And in some cases, repeated inability to obtain the arousal may result in a psychological backlash, a mental block, which further inhibits progress.

The brain is the most complex and powerful sex organ of all, but it is beyond the scope of this book to address the psychological aspects of making love. It should not be forgotten that for sex to be truly perfect there must be an integration of the physical, emotional and psychological aspects. But the fact is there are proven health and sexual benefits which occur from developing pelvic muscle tone. So doing these exercises can at least help, if not dramatically heighten sexual functioning. Many case studies have shown that improved tone and strength works wonders in stimulating a woman during sex. If you do have difficulties with sexual arousal, improvements on the physical side will allow you to focus on the psychological and emotional sides.

ORGASM DURING INTERCOURSE

The focus of this book is to show you a way to strengthen the pelvic floor muscles in order to improve their general functioning health. *All* women can surely benefit from the increased sensitivity to sexual stimulus. You can feel more aroused during all types of sexual activity – including manual and oral stimulation during homosexual or heterosexual love-making. But the focus here is on improving orgasmic ability and pleasure during sexual intercourse, since a great many women have trouble achieving orgasm specifically from this practice. These Sex Squeezes will literally make you fit for pleasure. By teaching you a way to keep your sex organs in healthy functioning order, when the other variables are present – love, attraction, security, respect, and the right mental stimulus – the sex you experience will be the best that it can be.

CHAPTER TWO

The Lost Secret

Although the idea of improving sex just by exercising the love muscles seems like a revolutionary finding, it's not. It's only in Western civilization that this secret appears to have been lost. The practice is centuries old. Traditional love texts as far back as 800 BC, from China, and later in Ancient Arabia and India, advocated the method as a way of prolonging sexual ecstasy. Indeed, those who saw sex more as a spiritual union than a physical act believed that muscle contraction within intercourse would generate life energy to revitalize two lovers. Some believed that tight pelvic floor muscles could prevent the body's life energy from leaking.

Different cultures described the action of manipulating the pelvic floor muscles in order to enhance the sensations.

The famed *Kama Sutra* is the Indian classic on the art of love-making. In it the author describes a sexual position called 'The Pair of Tongs'. Here the woman holds the man's lingam (penis) in her yoni (vulva). With her muscles she draws it in, presses upon it and keeps it inside for a long time.

The *Ananga Ranga* is another love manuscript from India which was later translated for the Arab world. The author describes a form of love-making in which the woman 'holds' the man and then 'milks' him by squeezing her yoni.

The Perfumed Garden written in sixteenth-century Arabia describes a movement called 'the boxing up of love'. Said to be the best of all the movements, those which women prefer to any other kind, the man penetrates deeply whereupon the woman seizes his member with her muscles. Their mutual caresses are said to provoke prompt orgasm with both the man and woman.

Even today the art of vaginal manipulation is still practised in cultures around the world, including Japan, Thailand and other countries in the Far East as well some African tribes and in India. Followers of Tantra, a Hindu cult or way of life based on cosmic sexuality, attribute great power to the practice. Although many of their rituals are secret and must be taught by Tantric guides, their sexual technique involves a form of contraction of the pelvic floor muscles called Yoni-Mudra. This is said to concentrate and radiate the energies up the spine to the brain to attain a mystical sense of bliss.

SOLE MALE PLEASURE

The practice most definitely increases the pleasure for both men and women. It must be pointed out, however, that in societies where the role of women is subservient to the male, the exercises are for the sole purpose of male satisfaction. In his book about prostitution in South-East Asia, *Sex, Money and Morality*, Thanh-dam Truong writes, 'Whatever physical assets she [a prostitute, often under slave labour] may possess are used to produce pleasure for the clients while she derives no material rewards . . . the brothel owner collects all the benefits. Women must compete with each other and develop skills to attract clients.'

These 'skills' can be seen in sex shows in all parts of

Asia where women have developed amazing dexterity and strength in their vaginal muscles. They are able to use them to perform such feats as smoking a cigarette, shooting darts and propelling balls across a room. Also, by inserting a tampon-like object with a long string attached and having someone hold the string taut from the other end, the women do various tricks such as opening a bottle or peeling an apple. The strong muscles are used by prostitutes on their clients as well. In one technique, the typically small Asian woman sits astride her client. She clenches her muscles around his penis and proceeds to rotate 360 degrees, instead of the usual thrusting for stimulation. But the women develop these muscles for the purpose of pleasing their clients, not themselves.

In some Islamic and African cultures, too, the man's gratification is of primary importance. Although the women may practise these exercises and develop strong pelvic floor muscle tone, there is almost no sexual benefit to the women because a high percentage undergo genital mutilation. This practice, defended as a form of female circumcision, is nothing of the kind. It actually destroys a woman's sex organs and ability for pleasure. Clitoridectomy is the most common form of this operation where the clitoris is wholly or partially removed, often with a shard of broken glass, or an unsterilised hunting knife. Infibulation is even worse because it involves removing the clitoris, cutting the labia (the vaginal lips) and sewing the vulva together so only a slight hole remains. This operation can be performed at birth, or more often as an initiation rite when a girl hits puberty.

Obviously sexual function is not the real issue for genital mutilation is a violent form of physical subordination. Although Western governments and even the World Health Organisation have called for the abolishment of these practices, because they are often part of the culture's religious dogma they are continued. Also common in the

Middle East, in Africa alone an estimated 66 million women have been genitally mutilated. Although genital mutilation is illegal in most Western countries, like secret back-street abortions in the 30s and 40s, cases even in Britain and the US have been reported in recent years.

So even though vaginal exercises to improve the sensation for men may be practised in other cultures, it would be wrong to consider them as a complement to love-making for a woman. No woman could enjoy sex in this context. In her book, *Women of Africa*, Maria Rosa Cutrufelli relates one woman's comments, 'To me it doesn't make much difference if my husband hits me on the face or has sex with me.'

The exercises in this book are meant to enhance *your* pleasure as a woman. While they will also please your partner, any references to this are not meant to be taken in any sort of a sexist context. For centuries, women have been used for men's pleasure rather than allowed or even encouraged to find their own. Fortunately, in our civilised Western environment the scenario is different. Men now understand that unless a woman fully enjoys herself, sex for her caring partner will be less than totally satisfying. The exercises in this book are meant to enhance the sexual experience of a man and woman in a loving, respectful relationship.

Read on to learn more about the age-old-turned-modern tradition of Sex Squeezes which will lead you on the path to erotic ecstasy.

CHAPTER THREE

Love Muscles

Although sexology in the West is a new phenomenon, sex was studied and recorded in ancient lore centuries ago. For example, in ancient China, The Tao was a philosophy of living that permeated the culture. Among its beliefs was the principle of equilibrium in the universe. This extended to love-making. They viewed sex as a balancing of the female energy, yin, and the male energy, yang. Explicit books on the topic described ways of regulating and regenerating this life force. The Taoists noted what would be scientifically recognised a millennium later – the different phases of sexual arousal in a man and woman.

In *The Tao of Love and Sex*, Jolan Chang discusses the Taoist stages of female satisfaction. The first stages of arousal are carefully described. 'Her face is flushing red and her ears are hot. This indicates that thoughts of making love are active in her mind . . . Her nose is sweaty and her nipples become hard. This signifies that the fire of her lust is somewhat heightened. The man should wait for her lust to intensify before going in deeper . . . Her red ball (vulva) is richly lubricated and her fire of lust is nearing its peak . . .'

While these observations were based purely on intense visual scrutiny, they keenly match the more technical recordings tabulated with advanced medical equipment within the past forty years.

Centuries later, researchers Masters and Johnson identified a similar pattern of sexual response in a woman.
They found that while men tended to have fairly predictable sexual response pattern, women seemed to have an
infinite variety which could vary with respect to intensity
and duration. Multiple orgasms were characterised by
a series of recurring orgasmic experiences with no
recordable plateau phase intervals in between, or by a
single, long continued orgasmic episode, each of which
could last up to sixty seconds.

THE STAGES OF SEXUAL AROUSAL

In their classic text, *Human Sexual Response*, Masters
and Johnson noted that during the Excitement phase a
woman experiences a sex flush over her face, breasts
and later other areas of the body. Nipples become
hard and there is immediate vaginal lubrication. The
clitoris swells and elongates. During this phase, from
the first thirty seconds after a man starts thrusting, the
inner two-thirds of the vagina involuntarily expands. It
actually lengthens and widens. In fact, it overexpands
so much that a fully erect penis can feel lost inside it.
As coital thrusting continues, after a minute or so, the
ballooning subsides. The vagina involuntarily contracts
around the penis. Although these slight adjustments mean
a woman can comfortably accommodate small and larger
penises, clearly – at least with the muscles at the entrance
to the vagina – stronger muscles can mean a snugger fit.
This provides more sensation for both partners.

During the Plateau phase, the areola around the nipples
swells creating an illusion that there has been a loss of nipple erection. Heart rate elevates and the clitoris retracts,
becoming difficult to observe. The minor labia (inner

lips) become deep red and may also swell to twice their normal size. Although the inner vagina has expanded, increased blood flow causes the outer third of the vagina to swell and form what is called the orgasmic platform. The entrance becomes smaller by 30 to 50 per cent. It is at this part of the vagina where most of the voluntary musculature is. So coupled with the swelling, stronger muscles can make the opening quite tight, causing some pretty intense stimulation for the penis.

Female Physical Reactions to Arousal

Excitement phase	sex flush on body; hardened nipples; vaginal lubrication; swollen, erect clitoris; expanding vagina
Plateau phase	entire nipple area swells; increased heart rate; clitoris retracts; inner vaginal lips swell and redden; outer vagina swells; increased overall muscle tension
Orgasmic phase	peak muscle tension as pelvic floor and uterus contract repeatedly
Resolution phase	nipple erection and sex flush subside; clitoris returns to normal position; vagina returns to normal size

---

The increasing muscle tension which has been accumulating in the first two phases comes to a peak during the Orgasmic phase. The vaginal muscles and the uterus contract explosively somewhere between three and fifteen times. A particularly high-intensity orgasm may launch with an initial contraction that lasts two to four seconds and subsequent contractions occurring at roughly one-second intervals.

Finally, the nipple erection and sex flush subside during the Resolution phase. The clitoris returns to its normal position within five to ten seconds after the cessation of orgasmic platform contractions.

Masters and Johnson noted, not surprisingly, that progression through these phases takes much longer in women than in men. This can be especially true during intercourse where there may not be sufficient stimulation, manually or orally or with an inexperienced man who doesn't know how to stimulate his partner. Interestingly, during masturbation when a woman is in control and knows exactly what to touch and for how long, she can climax, like a man, in as little as two or three minutes.

For a women to achieve a climax, she needs consistent stimulation of the clitoris. This causes a build-up of increased blood flow to the genitals and an increase in muscle tension which results in an orgasm. But if the stimuli are inadequate a woman may skip Orgasmic release and drop slowly from the Plateau phase into an excessively prolonged resolution phase. You have probably experienced this situation: you feel very aroused and on the brink of orgasm for an extended period, but have difficulty achieving a climax. If you or your partner tire, or stop, then not enough tension builds up. The result: no orgasm.

CARESSING THE C-SPOT

C-spot stimulation can be direct or indirect. While foreplay usually involves straightforward contact with a tongue or finger, intercourse offers only a few positions where you can zero in on the clitoris. In side-lying positions, the man or woman can easily stimulate the area with their hand. In 'doggy style' positions, manual stimulation is possible but maintaining balance at the same time can be tricky. In the most common pose, missionary-style man or woman on top, direct stimulation is nearly impossible. Compressed bodies leave little room for hand manoeuvres. Sometimes the man on top can grind his pelvis against the clitoris, or the woman on top can manipulate herself into a position where she rubs against him. However, this is not possible for every couple since body sizes and thrusting styles differ and affect the success of this type of stimulation. There lies the problem for many women who have difficulty with orgasm during intercourse. Thrusting may feel pleasurable, but often there is simply not contact with the C-spot to bring a woman to orgasm.

Direct stimulation of the clitoris may not always be necessary, however. Many women have found that secondary stimulus, or indirect contact with the clitoris, can build sufficient sexual tension. But this is where strong pelvic floor muscles can make a crucial difference in continued sexual arousal.

The success of indirect stimulation is largely dependent upon strong muscle tone. When there is full penetration by the penis and active thrusting, the friction affects the clitoris. As the penis penetrates deeply it stretches the skin around the vagina. As it withdraws, the skin returns to a more flacid state. This repetitive push and pull can move the clitoris up and down. Tight muscles provide more resistance, and therefore more stretch during penetration. Well-developed muscles can enhance these pleasure sensations so mounting sexual tension can continue.

STRONGER MUSCLES MEAN BETTER SEX

If the vaginal outlet is too expanded due to weak muscles there is less traction. The penis moves in and out, but with a negligible push-pull effect on the C-spot. So little, if any, secondary stimulation occurs. In *Love Play*, Dr David Delvin describes a spot he calls the S-zone at the opening to the vagina. Women like to be stretched, he claims, and may find it difficult to reach orgasm unless this zone is extended. He recommends several hand and finger techniques to stretch the area. If the theory is true, it may very well be because weak muscles which cause a wider opening provide less resistance, less friction and therefore decreased sensitivity and C-spot stimulation. So stretching the area manually can produce more sensation. This shouldn't be necessary when the muscles remain strong and tight. Exercising these muscles to improve their tone can make the normal stretching provided by the penis adequate stimulation.

There are also other ways that strong pelvic floor muscles can improve sex. When you're aroused, blood-flow to the clitoris increases, giving you more sensation. So during sex, actively working your muscles pumps more blood into the area, enhancing the feeling.

Since the build-up of sexual excitement is related to increased levels of muscular tension, the fitter your muscles on the inside, the greater their ability to contract, or tense up.

In addition, the more control you have over your muscles, the easier you can manipulate your body during sex to a position that feels good. You can consciously increase or decrease the tension as necessary.

Sex Squeezes can:

- improve traction during thrusting to stimulate your C-spot
- increase pressure for more feeling when using a condom
- pump more blood into the area to enhance sensitivity
- increase sexual tension when you want to come
- decrease tension when you're not ready for him to do so
- make the same old sex positions much more interesting
- decrease symptoms of incontinence
- help strengthen tissues after childbirth
- keep ageing vaginal tissue younger.

ENHANCED MALE SENSATION

Men can also benefit from both their own and their partner's stronger pelvic floor muscles. The penis is more easily stimulated by a tighter vagina. Greater constriction at the entrance means more pressure as it goes in and out.

Different sex positions invariably feel looser or tighter. Since the vagina is actually a balloon-like structure, the muscles help gather and compress the tissue walls, forming a natural corrugation which you can feel by inserting a finger. As the vagina expands during arousal, the tissues smooth out. In roomier sexual positions where the legs are very wide apart and raised, for example, stronger muscles may help provide a snugger fit with a more agreeable sensation of fullness for the woman and more direct pressure and friction for the man.

Especially for those who find condoms less enjoyable than skin-to-skin contact, increased muscle tone can make the pressure firmer. Actively employing these muscles while using a condom will help increase the sensation for both partners.

FLEXING YOUR LOVE MUSCLES

Ageing, childbirth and the Western lifestyle of little activity and lots of passive sitting can cause these muscles to weaken considerably, even in younger women. If your muscles are weak at present, you will experience definite improvements from practising the Sex Squeezes. Even if your pelvic floor muscle tone is fine, you can still improve your health and enhance your sexual enjoyment. As with all muscles in the body, tone and strength can always be better. Doing the exercises *before* you have any problems is great preventative medicine. The exercise maxim that applies to getting fit is pertinent here too: *If you don't use it, you lose it*.

Let's look at exactly what you need to do.

CHAPTER FOUR

The Tightness Inside

Many women spend hours toning their bodies, but focus most on the outside and forget about the muscles inside. Surveys show that most women tend to exercise primarily to improve their looks and then to improve their health. Adding Sex Squeezes to your routine of jogging, step, abdominal crunches and bicep curls will enhance your healthy look, for within the brightly coloured leggings and shiny Lycra, you'll have a very sexy, strong vagina.

Even if you don't exercise regularly, you can begin to get fit from the inside out! Sex Squeezes are quite discreet so you can fit them into your normal routine. You can do them before or after brushing your teeth, while driving or during other daily activities. Think how much more fun (and productive) waiting in a queue is when you're secretly squeezing!

In order to work this area, you need to become familiar with your sex organs and the muscles around them. The next few pages get graphic by exploring the physiology of the gentials in detail. Taking an in-depth look at the pelvic floor muscles and how they work is obviously a clinical area. While it may seem very unsexy, it's difficult to master the exercise technique without thoroughly understanding what's going on. Though the end result is undoubtedly erotic, the exercises require discipline, concentration and sometimes monotonous action that is distinctly different from the fits of passion associated with sex. Some aspects of the exercise routine can seem to sterilise love-making and turn it into a carefully calculated act of muscle contraction and prescribed movement. Like any subject, learning more about it increases what you get out of it. The more you know, the more you will appreciate the nuances. If you keep your mind closed to new perspectives you can easily fall into habitual patterns. These are what cause making love with the same partner to grow old and stale. In fact, learning how all the body parts function can be fascinating because the body is truly a work of art. With sex, the more you prepare and the more you understand, the more you will be able to satisfy yourself and your partner. Achieving this control will also bring sexual self-confidence to women who feel insecure. You'll gain the all-important psychological edge – ultimately the most important factor for fantastic sex.

The fact is that you can be diligent about your exercises and their technique at times when love-making is furthest from your mind. When you are in a state of lustful desire in the heat of the moment, this technical focus will go by the wayside. If you've done your preparation, it's at this moment when the exercises do their thing. An Olympic athlete can lose himself in the moment of his winning glory, despite the hard work he did to prepare. The muscle tone you've gained will improve your movement and control. You'll forget about the specifics and just exhilarate in the sensations they produce.

SEX ORGANS – SEX MUSCLES

The vulva is the name for the female sex organ which consists of the mons pubis (the fatty area of skin with pubic hair), the labia majora and minora (the inner and

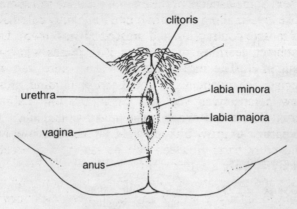

The structures of the vulva

outer vaginal lips), the vagina (the tube which gives access to the cervix and uterus), the clitoris (the pleasure organ at the top junction of the inner lips), the urethral orifice (where urine is expelled), and associated glands and other structures.

This area, along with the anal area, is protected by sheaths of muscle fibres. Known as the pelvic floor, or perineum, there are a number of interconnected voluntary and involuntary muscles. Each opening in this area (the urethra for urination, the vagina, and the anus) has its own sphincter muscle which keeps the holes constricted.

The Levator Ani muscle group is among the most important of the muscles for overall health because it actually provides support for various organs, including the vagina, bladder, colon, and uterus. The medial part of this muscle is known as the pubococcygeus, or the PC muscle. These muscles literally help to hold everything in its proper place. Especially during standing, they counter-effect the pull of gravity which can make your organs drop.

Muscles of the Pelvic Floor

Voluntary Muscles	Function
Sphincter urethra	muscles which constrict the urinary opening
Ischiocavernosus	insert into the side of the clitoris
Bulbospongiosus	connects to the erectile tissue of the clitoris
Bulbocavernosus	connects to the erectile tissue of the clitoris
Transverse perineal	joins with sphincter ani and the sphincter vaginae
Erector clitoridus	helps keep clitoris erect
Sphincter vaginae	constricts the vaginal opening; contributes to erection of clitoris
Levator ani – pubococcygeus (pc) and iliococcygeus (ic)	ic supports lower end of rectum, bladder & pc supports vagina and surrounds vagina like a loop so it is sphincteric
Sphincter ani externus	usually relaxes during defecation, otherwise keeps orifice closed

The table above shows most of the voluntary muscles in the perineum, that is, the ones that you can actively exercise. Most of the voluntary muscle is in the pelvic floor and it is this area which is most active during sex. During an orgasm there is an involuntary contraction of the entire perineal body, the outer third of the vagina, the rectum and the lower abdomen. But the transverse perineal muscle, the bulbocavernosus group, the sphincter ani external and the lower portion of the rectus abdominus are the muscles which most actively respond. The levator ani and ischiocavernosus muscles contribute to the orgasmic platform developed in the outer third of the vaginal. As you may recall from

Chapter 3, the entrance to the vagina swells during the Plateau phase of arousal.

Because these muscles are interconnected, when you exercise one, you usually exercise others. Once you develop a degree of muscular control, however, you may be able to isolate them somewhat to work them more specifically. Keeping all the sex muscles toned can improve their contractibility and efficiency.

HOW THESE MUSCLES BECOME WEAK

Starting as young as twenty-five years old, the ageing process can cause the loss of vital muscle mass in all muscles, including the pelvic floor in women. There is also a reduction in speed, strength and duration of muscle contraction. There is a loss of lubrication, particularly

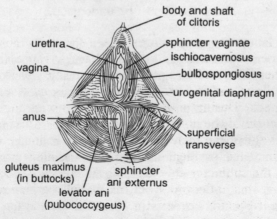

The pelvic floor muscles

after menopause. If you're poorly lubricated, the friction during sex (or at any other time) can make you sore or more prone to infection.

Symptoms of weakness in this area may include general pelvic fatigue and a sense of heaviness in the pelvis. Some women have a lack of sensation or numbness. There may also be a loss of urine when you laugh, cough, sneeze or exert yourself in some way.

One might think that if you do regular exercise like walking or cycling and have a fairly strong, healthy body, you would naturally have strong pelvic floor muscles. This is not necessarily the case, since exercise is specific. Just as a marathon runner or ballet dancer may have well-developed legs, but a weak upper body, you may not be as strong if you do only aerobics, for example, and no specific pelvic floor exercises. One recent study showed that 48 per cent of women in a group who exercised regularly experienced urine leakage when they laughed, coughed or sneezed. Incontinence is usually associated with weak pelvic floor muscles. Muscles grow weak with disuse; unless you exercise them, no matter how active your lifestyle, they could still be underused.

Exercising the muscles before you develop a weakness, or even before pregnancy has many benefits. Since so many women have problems just locating the muscles in order to work them, if you wait until there is already a weakness present, you are doubly impaired. Learning how to do them properly while pregnant can be hard work because of a hormone which relaxes everything you're trying to contract. Learning early means you can maintain your muscle strength throughout your life, creating a good level of fitness and possibly reducing the incidence of future problems – and of course, your sex life will be improved.

Even if you are currently pregnant, or are starting this training later in your life, you can still see dramatic improvements. In fact, most of the studies done have been on women like you and there is no doubt that you can reap the rewards of improved vaginal health and enhanced sexual response.

Pregnancy

No matter how strong they are before the big event, the pelvic floor muscles are inevitably weakened during childbirth. Babies are big things! Some muscle fibres may be torn and nerves may be separated from the muscle cells. These muscles can lose elasticity. The damage to the nerves may cause a loss of sensation. The size of the baby, the size of the pelvis, the length of labour and the original state of the perineal muscles before pregnancy all play a part in determining the extent to which this area will be injured. During sexual arousal, when the vagina naturally expands, these tissues may overexpand to such an extent that there is no discernible constriction and therefore less stimuli for the woman and her partner.

The most serious injuries occur near the opening of the vagina since it's the smallest part. Of course with it's contractile function during orgasm, constricting to offer sexual friction and traction, it's easy to see how sex after having children can be less enjoyable than before. But in the worst cases, these muscles become so lax that the contents of the pelvis are not supported properly. Then they push into the bladder, often causing stress incontinence, or urine leakage. The organs can prolapse, or a hernia can appear on the weak vaginal wall.

The good news is that this tissue has amazing recuperative ability. Not every muscle cell becomes injured and those that are not will work out the weaker ones because they are all interconnected. Some of the muscle cells may even establish new nerve attachments, since a single nerve fibre is capable of growing to supply an increasing number of muscle cells. But total healing doesn't happen on its own. Unless specific exercises are done, not much of the area will recover. To help regain pre-birth strength and elasticity, pelvic floor exercises should be done for at least six months after childbirth.

The best preparation for labour is regular Kegel exercises to establish good muscle tone. You regain more elasticity after birth if these muscles are toned to begin with because fit muscles recover better. This may also help to prevent incontinence after birth. Although strengthening the muscles before birth makes sense in terms of recovery, you might assume that heavily toned muscles might inhibit the expansion of the vagina during birth. This is not the case for two reasons.

First of all, the natural hormonal processes during pregnancy make the muscle fibres more elastic, regardless of their original tone. Secondly, when muscles are actively strengthened in their full range of motion, that is, when you work them by both a full contraction and a full release for each repetition, the muscle also gains significant flexibility, even if it is not actively stretched. It is more contractile, and it can stretch and contract with greater ease.

One observation made by Masters and Johnson may be interesting for women trying to conceive. Part of the vaginal expansion resulting from a woman's arousal creates an indentation just under the cervix. When the male ejaculates inside, the semen tends to pool into this curve. When a woman has good muscle tone in the PC muscle, the Orgasmic platform that swells and constricts the vaginal opening helps keep the sperm inside rather than flowing out of the vagina.

Menopause

The hormonal changes associated with the menopause

affect sexual functioning. The cessation of oestrogen causes the vaginal tissues to become less lubricated, thinner and smoother. During sexual arousal, the vagina loses some of its expansive ability. It takes a longer time to lubricate, and there is less lubrication. General tension of the muscles also decreases.

Doing pelvic floor exercises can't totally counteract the changes associated with ageing, but they can certainly help. Muscle mass can be increased and therefore so can contractile and tension-building ability – which is especially important for orgasm. Of course regular sex can keep the muscles in good shape, too. Masters and Johnson found that several women they studied who'd had active sex once or twice a week most of their adult lives, even in their sixties and seventies, had the lubricating and orgasmic contraction abilities of women half their age. Good news! Start those Sex Squeezes now!

Incontinence

Urinary incontinence is the involuntary leakage of urine upon any exertion. Not surprisingly, one gynaecologist reported that women in the Far East seem to have a lower incidence of incontinence probably due to the more common practise of pelvic floor exercise. Incontinence is very common in Western women. Surveys have shown that up to half of young women have experienced it at one time or another and 16 per cent suffer daily. It can happen when you cough, laugh, sneeze, lift something heavy, or even during high-impact exercise like running or aerobics.

For some sufferers, incontinence can result in a lack of sensation or leakage during sexual intercourse. Unless the muscles are strengthened the leaks will continue –

perhaps even getting worse – as unused muscles weaken.
When incontinence is the result of weak pelvic floor
muscles, it can be significantly improved, or even cured,
with Kegel exercises. There have even been cases of
women who have had unsuccessful operations in order
to treat the problem and later found that these exercises
alone corrected it.

Small weights can be inserted into the vagina to give
the muscles a more strenuous workout. Often, the lack of
sensation and muscle control that accompany weak pelvic
floor muscles make it difficult to exercise the area. The
physical stimulation of the weights helps women to focus
on the appropriate muscles to squeeze, which makes them
doubly effective. You'll find out where to purchase the
weights and how to use them later in the book.

DON'T WAIT TILL IT'S TOO LATE

Kegel exercises, pelvic push-ups, Sex Squeezes – whatever you want to call them – can not only enhance your
sex life, but they are a preventative health measure which
gynaecologists internationally recommend for *all* women
regardless of age.

CHAPTER FIVE

Muscle Manipulation

Who would ever have thought that muscles were such a big deal? Dr Kegel realised it when he found that out of 3000 women he studied, those with strong perineal musculature of a certain measurable degree of strength had few sexual complaints. But the women with thin weak muscles frequently expressed indifference or dissatisfaction with sexual activity. They often had no sensation or didn't like the sensation they had. Following restoration of the pelvic floor muscles, many of them experienced orgasm for the first time. This led him to conclude that sexual feeling within the vagina is closely related to muscle tone, and that it can be improved through muscle education and resistance exercise.

A strong muscle is a toned muscle. A strong muscle generally has more mass, so having more muscle or at least better-conditioned muscle, means it will function better. It will be more elastic, stronger, more extensible and more contractile – all the things desirable in a healthy, sexy pelvic floor.

So let's take a look at how you can manipulate a muscle through exercise to train it do what you need it to do.

HOW YOUR MUSCLES WORK

Research has shown that strengthening specific muscles is as important as regular, all-round, aerobic exercise. Ageing causes a loss of up to a half pound of muscle per decade. This means a slower metabolism – and easier weight gain because muscle is active tissue. The more you have, the higher your metabolism. If you lose it, your metabolism lowers proportionately. It is therefore easy to gain weight for no apparent reason. Strength training is essential to the body. By investing twenty minutes, just twice a week, performing sensible resistance exercises you can *reverse* many aspects of the ageing process as well as make many other improvements.

Not only will you increase the stability of your joints and help prevent osteoporosis (weakening of the bones), finely tuned muscles will improve your posture and coordination so you move with more grace and precision. In addition, strength training can lower your blood pressure, blood cholesterol and even help reduce the need for insulin in Type 2 diabetes. You can thwart the natural loss of muscle caused by ageing. You'll feel younger, look younger and function better.

Considering how strong muscles affect your entire body, it's not surprising that they can benefit your sexual health and functioning.

HOW TO TONE, STRENGTHEN AND TIGHTEN

The most effective way to train your muscles is to overload them with resistance. When a muscle cell is worked at a level just beyond that to which it is accustomed, it is forced to work harder. In doing so tiny microtears are made in the muscle fibres. Within approximately forty-eight hours of rest they heal, re-build and grow stronger.

Your muscles adapt to the extra challenge by developing more strength (the amount of force a muscle can produce) and more endurance (the ability to contract repeatedly over a period of time). Appearance changes, too, as you develop more muscle tone (how firm a muscle is) and definition (how sculpted it looks).

You can develop a certain amount of tone by doing any exercise. But since muscles increase in strength in direct proportion to the demands placed upon them, the firmer and stronger you want to be, the more resistance you need to use so the muscles work harder. There are many types of resistance available. The most common are weight machines (as you would see in the gym), free weights (dumbbells and weighted bars), and elastic bands.

Applying these principles to the pelvic floor muscles means doing specific exercises to make them work so they'll be stimulated to stay strong. Doing *only* Kegel exercises at a minimum intensity for a minimum amount of time means you'll probably just improve their overall endurance, rather than elicit major gains in strength. They will be able to contract for longer periods without getting fatigued and will probably maintain a reasonable degree of tone. This is sufficient for general pelvic support; for instance, to recover from childbirth or to help problems that arise from weak musculature. But sex being more active demands the use of more of the muscles, so they need to be exercised harder to become stronger.

To increase their strength you need to increase the intensity of the Kegel exercises by squeezing extra hard, holding a squeeze for extra long, or using some type of resistance. The vaginal dumbbells mentioned earlier are small weights which come in different sizes, so you can control the amount you use very precisely. Once you can hold a weight in for a certain length of time, you can progress to a heavier weight.

With any exercise, the amount of weight you lift and the number of repetitions you do will determine whether you develop more strength or more endurance in your muscles. The general rule is to use heavier weights with lower repetitions to build strength and bulk, and to use lighter weights with higher repetitions to build endurance.

TYPES OF MUSCLE

Another consideration when you train your muscles is what kind of muscle you are training. There are two basic muscle-fibre types known as fast twitch and slow twitch. All muscles contain both kinds, including the pelvic floor group. Each play a separate role when movement is required.

Fast twitch fibres are responsible for powerful, fast action. Any maximal efforts will call upon these cells in a muscle to work. Slow-twitch fibres, on the other hand, perform the lower intensity, longer-lasting work. A marathon runner might develop more of his slow-twitch fibres. A sprinter will develop more fast-twitch.

To strengthen the pelvic floor muscles thoroughly, both types of fibre must be conditioned. This is achieved by varying the intensity of the exercises. When a muscle contracts, first the slow twitch fibres are activated. Since fast twitches are only employed when maximum effort is required, you must keep repeating the contraction at maximum speed or at maximum tension. As you will notice when you start doing the Sex Squeezes, you will do some with weights, some quick and fast, some slow and long, and everything in between. That will guarantee that you prepare your sex muscles for the inevitable variations you will encounter during love-making. Good sex usually lasts, so you want to develop muscle stamina in the slow-twitch fibres. But when the passion hits you, or when you're practising some of your erotic exercises, you might need extra strength, and extra power. Training your fast-twitch fibres will keep you primed for action.

MUSCLE COORDINATION

One final aspect of muscle conditioning that plays an important role in your sex training is the development of muscle coordination. When you exercise, not only do you strengthen your muscles, you improve the way the nerves and fibres coordinate messages from your brain.

A muscle has thousands of muscle fibres. Each individual nerve is connected to a group of muscle fibres and this is known as a motor unit. They contract in groups, rather than individually. If you require a lot of strength, as you might when you lift a heavy weight, or perhaps during a very strong orgasmic contraction, you will use many motor units in a muscle. Smaller moves use fewer motor units.

Coarse movements use a greater number of motor units since they usually involve more strength. When you develop your sex muscles, learning to squeeze strongly will help you utilize as many motor units as possible. But once you have gained a certain amount of control, you can develop more precise muscle action. This means you can learn how to squeeze different areas of the same muscle. Or you can vary the speed and rhythm at which you squeeze to add variety in a sexual position. You are basically fine-tuning your muscles – executing the skilful movement of a ballerina as opposed to exerting the brute force of a rugby player.

The women in the Far East who are able to perform highly skilled sex acts are able to do so because they have developed both a great deal of strength and incredibly precise muscle control. One particular sex trick performed involves a woman inserting a dildo-like object inside herself. A rope is attached to it. She ties the end to a cart, puts one of her voyeurs inside of it, grips her vaginal muscles tight and pulls the cart around. A Japanese sex trick, which displays the mastery of specific motor skills, shows a woman gripping a pen inside herself, and then writing messages of good luck for the admiring crowd. Not necessarily acts to aspire to, but evidence of the incredible muscle strength that can be achieved.

IS SEX ENOUGH?

Since orgasms cause the muscles to contract there is some evidence to suggest that a regular sex life or regular masturbation keeps your sex muscles in condition. 'Regular' means roughly three times a week. If there's any existing weakness, then the Kegels need to be done to supplement the sex. Since the muscle contraction during sex is involuntary, many women may not develop keen muscle awareness so it's important not to rely on sex alone, but to perform voluntary contractions by doing the exercises as well.

As you'll see in the fitness programme, once you've developed an adequate amount of strength in your pelvic floor muscles, you can decrease the time spent doing them to a minimum of seven minutes a day, a few times a week, in order to maintain the musculature. Studies have shown that the amount of exercise you do can be decreased significantly once you've reached a desired fitness level, as long as your sessions are fairly intense when you do work out.

RESULTS

Although there are improvements in efficiency, strength and mass within the first few weeks of exercising your muscles, it usually takes about twelve weeks to see measurable gains. The results depend upon the level of strength you started with, how hard you work and with how much resistance. Typical Kegel exercises are said to show improvements in strength and tone after about three months. Since the Sex Squeezes I've devised are of a considerably higher intensity, you may feel stronger much sooner. Generally the weaker you are the more room there is for improvement, so you'll see results fast.

Now you're ready to start squeezing . . .

CHAPTER SIX

Sex Squeezes

Your first step in training is to understand the basics. Surprise: you're going to learn how to squeeze. It sounds simple, but for many women, squeezing the pelvic floor muscles is a bit like wiggling your ear: you can do it if you find the muscle to move, but where is the muscle? The muscles are there but if you've never really focused on their sensation before, finding them may take a bit of time. Once you've found them, though, they won't get lost again.

There are different ways to locate your pelvic floor muscles. When you've found them once you'll train your brain to record their position and note what nerves to access to put them into action. The focusing exercises I give you mean you'll practise different ways to locate the appropriate muscles. Constant repetition increases the probability that you can find them again easily. You're essentially teaching your brain to memorize the nerve path which activates a certain muscle, or part of a muscle. This makes it easier to move muscles in a particular way at will.

Dr Kegel categorized this training as being comprised of four phases. Phase one is the period required for general awareness and coordination of the muscles. You may find the muscles right away, or with daily attempts take as long as a week to recognize them. The second phase is transitional. Here you can confidently activate the desired muscles. The third stage occurs when you start reaping the benefits – the muscles contract more strongly and you may experience a relief of some of your symptoms – if you're treating incontinence, for example. The final phase shows marked increase in strength and control. You can perform the moves with less fatigue. The muscles have become firmer, thicker and broader, with improved function.

You will be going through six levels in the following pelvic floor training programme. Once you identify the muscles, you'll learn the basic Kegel. Since we're going for optimum, rather than minimum levels of pelvic floor strength and coordination, you'll make your skills sports-specific by doing various Sex Squeezes, Power Squeezes and Rhythm Squeezes. Finally you'll take your Sex Squeezes into the bedroom, practise with your partner and incorporate them into your nights (or days) of passion.

The Programme

Look at the chart on pages 50–51 for a quick glance at the programme to develop strength, endurance and control in your love muscles. Here is a detailed description of each step.

1. Choose whether you will follow Plan 1 or Plan 2.
2. Start at Level one and practise the recommended exercises as instructed. You may find it difficult to do this much at the beginning. If this is the case, then start with three or four minutes and gradually increase. Once you can do seven minutes easily, progress to the exercises at the next level. Again, you may need to begin with less than are indicated, but work up to the level and keep practising until you have improved enough to meet the goal of that level. Once you have, proceed to the next, and so on.

Level One
Find a time and space where you are unlikely to be interrupted. Practise each of the focusing exercises described in Chapter 6 which include observation, visualization, interruption and isolation. Do these for a total of seven minutes each day. You should be able to identify how to work the muscles correctly within a week. If you have difficulties, invest in a pair of vaginal weights (see Appendix) which will help you to target the right muscles.

Level Two
Do your basic Kegel exercise every day (see Chapter 6). Depending upon which plan you are following, practise holding the squeeze without releasing for 10–30 seconds a time. Also practice controlled squeeze and releases starting with 100–150 times a session and working up to 300 times consecutively twice a day. Remember, you may very well find it impossible to do 100 straight away. Start with 20 and aim to increase the number of squeezes you do every time you exercise. Then keep practising until you can do the required number. Also

THE PROGRAMME

	Women Plan 1	Women with children Plan 2	Goal progress to next level once you can do this
Level one Focusing	observation visualization interruption isolation	observation visualization interruption isolation	squeeze the PC muscles and anus separately
Time	*7 minutes per day*	*7 minutes per day*	*7 minutes per day*
Level two The Kegel Exercise	hold-squeeze for 30 secs squeeze-release 150 times	hold-squeeze for 10 secs squeeze-release 110 times	hold-squeeze for 60 secs squeeze-release 300 times
Time	*twice daily*	*twice daily*	*twice daily*
Level three Sex Squeezes	do the advanced postures and rhythms every other day.		start with the beginning, then move to the advanced postures and rhythms every day.
Time	*every other day*	*every other day*	*every other day*

	Women Plan 1	Women with children Plan 2	Goal progress to next level once you can do this
Level four Power Squeezes	hold each repetition for 30 to 90 secs. do 15 repetitions	hold each repetition for 30 to 90 secs. do 12 repetitions	hold each repetition for 90 secs. do 3 sets of 12 repetitions
Time	*3 times per week*	*3 times per week*	*3 times per week*
Level five Rhythm Squeezes	practise 4 of the exercises each session: vary the squeezes you choose		
Time	*twice a week*	*twice a week*	*twice a week*
Level six Sexercises	Your Choice!	Get Creative!	Get Passionate!
Level seven Maintenance	choose your favourite exercises alternating between Sex, Power and Rhythm Squeezes		
Time	*7 minutes, 3 times a week*	*7 minutes, 3 times a week*	*7 minutes, 3 times a week*

practise the static hold until you can maintain a squeeze for 60 seconds without relaxing the pelvic floor muscles.

Level Three

Go through the five beginning postures in Chapter 6 and practise squeezing in each position. Then practise each of the beginning rhythms in each of the postures. Do these every day. Once you can go through these quite easily and you feel you have a good deal of control, progress to the advanced postures and rhythms. Practise the advanced exercises every other day. When you can perform the number of repetitions indicated for each exercise, progress to the next level.

Level Four

Practise your Power Squeezes in Chapter 7, ideally with one of the resistance tools described (see Appendix). Do each of the exercises as indicated. Try to contract with as much force as you can during each squeeze. Once you can do the basic exercises, try to do them and hold each squeeze for 30–90 seconds before you release it. Do these every other day. When you can do three separate sets of twelve repetitions of these strong power holds, progress to the next level.

Level Five

Go through the visualization exercises in Chapter 8. Practise these until you can consciously control different areas of the pelvic musculature. When you feel confident that you can manipulate the muscles to move in subtle ways, use your partner or a resistance tool to practise the Rhythm Squeezes in Chapter 9. Try four different exercises each session, twice a week. When you can effectively replicate the different squeeze patterns, move on to the next, most enjoyable level and apply your new strength and skill to love-making.

Level Six

You will have noticed by now which positions are most comfortable for you. You will have experienced a preference for one type of squeeze pattern over another. Go ahead and put your muscles to use here. Remember to learn just one or two exercises at first and learn them well. Once you've exhausted their possibilities try a few more moves. Enjoy!

Level Seven

When you are satisfied with the level of strength you have achieved in your love muscles you can go to maintenance mode of practising your favourite exercises for seven minutes, just three times a week. Alternate between the various sex, power and rhythm squeezes. You may be tempted to stop exercising altogether, but remember these exercises are still needed to maintain good functioning of the muscles, so by all means, decrease the time you spend but keep them a habitual part of your life.

The best results from any type of exercise (running, tennis and other activities) are produced when there is intense, regular training. But there is a fine line between doing enough to see fairly quick results, and doing too much so that the task seems overwhelming. If an exercise programme takes too much time and effort, then most people simply won't stick to it. To be as user-friendly as possible, this programme takes both aspects into account. The exercises have been designed to be as effective as possible in the shortest amount of time, but the overall routine varies from level to level so that at times you'll be doing minimal effort and basic moves, and at other times you'll be working a little harder and with more precision.

To begin with, you'll do the basic exercises for just seven minutes a day. Then, as you increase your strength and interest, you'll increase the intensity to work a little harder for longer periods. To keep the workout interesting, the Sex Squeezes and Power Squeezes provide challenging variations on the basic exercise. Then you'll add a little excitement to your exercise regimen by bringing your partner into the picture. You'll practise your exercises on him, and finally use your skills to enhance your love-making technique. Once you've established a satisfactory amount of muscular strength and control, and are experiencing the benefits in the bedroom, you'll drop back down to the minimal amount of exercise required to maintain your muscle tone: seven minutes a day.

There are two different programmes: Plan 1 for women who have not had children, and a less intense programme, Plan 2, for women who have. If you have gone through labour you may need to progress more slowly to help build back the pelvic tone that was weakened from childbirth. Even if you had children many years ago, go ahead and follow Plan 2. You can always increase the intensity if you feel it's not enough.

The idea is for you to start at level one. Once you can achieve the goal, progress to the next higher level. Starting at Level two you will notice that you must increase the intensity of your exercises in order to meet the goal. The pace at which you do this can vary. Basically, if you can start off with the recommended number of contractions easily, go ahead and add a few more so that you push yourself a little each day.

In one report, Dr Arnold Kegel prescribes twenty to forty hours of progressive resistance exercise spread over twenty to sixty days in order to restore tone and function to lax or atrophied perineal muscles. Obviously, the weaker you are to begin with, the more work you need to do to establish a minimum healthy level of strength. The greater the resistance you use, the harder you work, and the quicker the results. Studies confirm that more intense exercises, or using the weights may be more efficient. Due to individual differences, some women will pass through these phases more quickly than others. Go at a pace which is comfortable for you.

If your muscles are not too weak to begin with, you may push yourself harder. The strength needed for sex is probably greater than that needed for overall healthy tone, so a more intense exercise regime may be more effective for sex.

Practise Makes Perfect

Like other kinds of workouts, the hardest part is actually doing the exercises. While you're reading this book and excited about the results you can achieve, you'll remember to do them. But long afterwards the impetus may leave you and you'll simply forget to do them at all. If you can establish the programme as a regular part of another daily activity, you'll benefit more than just relying on memory to do them. While it may be difficult to incorporate the exercises into your daily activities at first while you're in the developmental stages (you can't exactly lie on the floor at the post office and practise your postures!), once you are at level seven, the maintenance phase, then you can easily incorporate them into other activities, like driving, standing in a queue, while watching TV or brushing your teeth.

Strength, Endurance and Coordination

The overall programme includes specific training that will help you to develop different qualities in your muscles. The Sex Squeezes in level three work mainly on developing endurance, overall muscle tone and basic coordination. The Power Squeezes work on improving your strength and muscle mass. The Rhythm Squeezes work on your coordination and fine control over the muscles.

The different exercises will recruit the different types of muscle fibres that comprise the muscles. Your fast-twitch fibres will be activated during the Power Squeezes and also during the other types when you exert maximum effort by squeezing as hard as you can or by squeezing very fast. The slow-twitch fibres will work whenever you do the squeezes at an average intensity. They'll improve by repeated contractions, working for longer periods.

For the best results possible, exercise both the inside and outside of your body. The health and sexual benefits achieved from regular aerobic exercise and body conditioning should not be overlooked. Aim to do some type of endurance activity such as walking, running, cycling, swimming or aerobics three to five times per week for between fifteen and sixty minutes. If you're new to exercise, start slow and work your way up. Overall fitness will greatly enhance the benefits you experience doing the Sex Squeezes.

LEVEL ONE

Focusing to Squeeze

Here are four ways to help you identify the appropriate muscles to work. Go ahead and do them all. If you have trouble focusing, stick to the method which you find easiest to concentrate on.

Observation

Squat over a mirror or sit and hold one in front of you to inspect your sex organs. Spread apart your outer lips:

feel their texture. Find your clitoris. Notice the valleys and ridges of your inner lips. Spot the various openings – the urethra, vagina and anus.

Now insert a clean finger into your vagina. Feel how the smoothness on the outside soon becomes bumpy and corrugated inside. If you've ever inserted a diaphragm or some types of tampon, you will be familiar with these tissues. Many women have been conditioned to perceive the vulva as dirty. In reality it's one of the cleanest areas of the body. Your inspection should seem no different than looking inside your mouth at the gums, tonsils or your teeth.

Continue to probe around all the walls of your vagina. Try to recall what you've read so far and be aware of the changes that take place when you become aroused. You may already be noticing a bit of lubrication simply because of the manual stimulation.

Notice what you see and notice what you feel. Stamp this in your mind. Since it may be difficult to focus on the muscles inside in order to make them contract, it's helpful to create a mental image of the area. When you later go through your exercises, you'll have a more concrete picture of what you are trying to affect.

Now, do the finger test. Contract and squeeze as hard as you can around your finger. If you do not feel pressure on your finger but you still feel you are squeezing *something*, it may be that you are inadvertently squeezing other muscles like your abdominals, inner thighs or buttocks. It's important to relax those and isolate just the pelvic floor.

Try squeezing again. If you're not sure you're doing it correctly, don't worry. The next few exercises will reinforce all the right sensations.

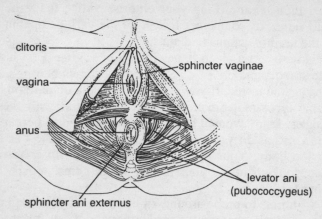

The female anatomy

Visualization

Now that you have an idea about what you look like, you need to take a deeper look inside. No, this does not mean getting a microscope, it means doing a bit of visualization with your inner eye so that you can focus on the different sensations your body produces.

Read this next section to get a general idea of what to do, or even better, record yourself reading it into a tape recorder. Then make yourself comfortable and lie on your back with your legs straight, arms by your sides. Make sure you are in a warm room. You may even want to put a blanket over yourself since your body will cool as it relaxes. Your clothing should be loose.

After you've done it once, go back through this exercise and at each area stop, initiate a strong muscle contraction and full release. This will help programme the mental sensation with the feeling and the action. Tense and relax as many areas as you can throughout your body. Notice the reactions to the skin, the muscle, observe any temperature changes, etc. This is a variation of a technique developed by a Harvard doctor, Herbert Benson, MD, called the Relaxation Response. As the name suggests, you'll not only develop your self-reflective abilities, you'll de-stress yourself at the same time.

Start breathing very slowly, in and out of your nose. Relax your hands, your toes, neck and forehead. Feel your body sinking into the floor. Now, starting from your feet, bring your mind's eye up your body slowly and stop to notice the different sensations you feel. Feel the clothing against your skin at certain points. Bring your focus on to the top of your big toe, along the front of your shin, to the top of the knee then travel around to key in on the back of the knee. Continue up your thigh and pause just a bit longer on your genitals. Focus on the labia. See if you can distinguish between the outer and inner lips. Move your focus to the vaginal opening. Remember what this area actually looks like and programme the picture and the feeling into your mind. Continue to travel around your pelvis, through your legs, up the inside of each thigh and then slide your eye around to your buttocks. Try to locate the anal opening and again move up to the vagina just to reinforce the difference in feeling. Travel up to the front to your clitoris. You may feel erotic sensations now – a slight tingle, an exaggerated pulse in the area. Now continue up your abdomen around each nipple to your neck and down your arms to your hands. Finally, bring your mind to your face and all around your head.

Repeat and perform a full contraction and release on every muscle you encounter.

Were you able to contract your pelvic floor muscles during

the second part of this exercise? Just to check, go ahead and reinsert a finger like you did during your observation. Try to squeeze. Can you do it? If you're not sure, don't worry. Read on.

Interruption

The most common way to begin to identify the muscles is to stop your urine flow when you are on the toilet – this is just a test to help focus on the muscles to squeeze. This actually activates the urethra sphincter, but since it is interconnected to the PC muscle, it's a good start. Do not do this too frequently. Instead focus on practising the other exercises to contract the vaginal area.

Isolation

Bring up your mental picture and recreate some scenes you've experienced in real life. Tighten your anus as if you are trying to stop the escape of wind. Then tighten your vagina as though you feel a tampon slipping out. Now, constrict the urethra as if you are holding in having to go to the toilet. Squeeze and release each. Hold all of them tight at once. Make sure surrounding muscles like the buttocks and abdomen stay relaxed.

If it's still difficult for you to find the right muscles to contract, you may have better luck using vaginal weights (see Appendix, page 119 for retailers.) One study found that it takes three times longer to learn the exercise alone as it does to do them with weights. This is because the weight gives you immediate feedback when it starts to fall out. The muscles respond almost on reflex to keep them in.

Practise these four focusing exercises until you can spot and contract the pelvic floor muscle at will. Once you can, there are a variety of rhythms, durations, numbers, intensities and positions in which you will squeeze. But one thing at a time. First, you need to build up a general degree of strength.

LEVEL TWO

The Kegel Exercise

This is the classic squeeze which is the basis for the rest of your workout. If you have done this before, go ahead and go through this exercise again, just to reinforce the basic technique. You can perform this exercise in any position, but you will probably find it most comfortable to sit or lie on your back.

> Tighten the pelvic floor muscles and hold the contraction for three to five seconds. Then relax completely. Breathe and place a hand on your abdomen during your next contraction to ensure that it is relaxed. You may wish to insert a finger or place your hand on top of your vagina so you can detect movement to confirm that you're squeezing the right muscles. Try to work up to holding the squeeze for ten seconds. Repeat this exercise fifteen to twenty times.

Most standard Kegel exercise routines prescribed by doctors and physiotherapists recommend doing fewer repetitions and sticking to the basic squeezes described without any of the more difficult variations. This is mostly for practical purposes. Since it's crucial that women do the exercises, they are more likely to do so if the routines are short and easy. In these cases, something is better than nothing at all, but to achieve significant increases in pelvic floor strength and muscle mass more quickly, it's more effective to do a challenging exercise routine.

So the following variations on the standard Kegels will help you progress to higher levels for better sex.

Note to Pregnant Women and New Mothers

For the first trimester you may do the Kegels lying down. After the fourth month, lying flat on your back is not recommended due to obstructed blood flow to the fetus, so do them in a standing or sitting position. If you have had an episiotomy, doing Kegels soon after delivery for six months will help to stimulate circulation to promote healing as well as improving muscle tone. Don't worry if you can't feel them right away; the area may be numb after delivery. Feeling will return to the perineum gradually over the next few weeks. Seek advice on the other types of exercises you should do to help recover.

LEVEL THREE

Sex Squeezes

Now you can get sex-specific and start training your pelvic floor muscles for sex. If you can look at sex for a minute as simply another physical activity such as tennis or swimming, you'll see that there are recognizable physical patterns and movements which are endemic to the 'sport'. We are going to use these exercises to improve these physical skills. The more skilful you are, the more you should get out of sex (on a physical level, that is).

Basically, you'll be trying to replicate all the positions into which your muscles may be moved, the rhythms at which they might contract, and the forces that they may exert (sometimes slow and easy, sometimes fast and powerful). If you remember from Chapter 5, one aspect of training is to programme new neuromuscular pathways or simply learn new ways of coordinating your muscles.

Breathing

The importance of breathing should not be overlooked, especially when you start doing Power Squeezes which exert much more force. Any time you contract a muscle and hold your breath you can inadvertently raise your blood pressure. This is due to the effort which can cause an increase in internal body pressure which causes an increase in blood pressure. Normally the rise is slight and should not be a problem, but if you have high blood pressure, check with your doctor first to ensure that you can safely follow this, or any other type of exercise. Many types of exercise have been shown to reduce blood pressure, but always check first.

Avoid holding your breath, try to breathe normally and relax. Exhale when you exert the force. If you find the exercises easier to do when your hold your breath then to break that pattern count aloud as you contract. Then switch the pattern of your breath and practise squeezing when you inhale and relaxing as you inhale. Then practise your squeezes a little faster, contracting not in coordination with your breathing. Continue to breathe throughout, rather than holding your breath.

1. Perform each of the beginning squeeze rhythms described while you are in each of the beginning postures as shown on the following pages. Some positions will be much easier to squeeze in than others. This is natural because different leg positions

will affect the resistance and range of motion of the exercise.

Beginning Postures

- **Sitting squeeze**. While sitting in a chair with your knees bent and wide apart, contract and relax your pelvic floor muscles practising each of the beginning rhythms described below.
- **Missionary squeeze**. While lying on your back with your knees bent into your chest and wide apart, contract and relax.
- **Split squeeze**. Lie on your back and hold a bent knee into your chest. Keep your other leg straight. Contract and relax, then switch legs.
- **Side squeeze**. Lie on one side and extend your top leg out directly in front of your hips. Prop your leg on a pillow to raise it slightly. Keep your bottom leg straight, with your knee slightly bent. Contract and relax, then switch sides.
- **Straddle squeeze**. Sit with your legs wide apart, knees slightly bent. Lean your chest slightly forward but keep your lower back straight. You will also stretch your inner thigh muscles in this position which will give you greater flexibility during sex. If these muscles hurt, bring your legs closer together.

Sitting Squeeze

Missionary

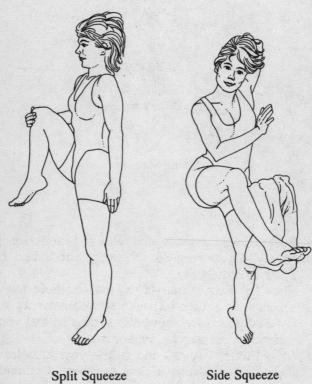

Split Squeeze   Side Squeeze

Straddle

Beginning Rhythms

- **Basic Boogie**. Contract and relax at a moderate speed twenty times. Progress to faster speeds and faster intervals in between.
- **Slow 'n' Easy**. Contract the muscle; hold for three seconds then relax for three seconds, twenty times. Gradually increase your holding time so that you can maintain a squeeze for ten seconds.
- **Slow Pump**. Contract and release your muscles as if you were simulating a slow heartbeat. Continue for three minutes.
- **Pump at Speed**. Speed up your 'slow pump' contractions. Make sure to release each one completely before squeezing again. Continue for three minutes.
- **Flutter**. Flutter the vaginal muscles by doing the

exercise faster with few pauses in between. Continue the flutters for as long as you can. Do five sets of them.

2. The advanced postures incorporate moves which use more movement and gravitational resistance. Perform the squeeze rhythms while you are in each of the advanced postures.

Advanced Postures

- **Stand in Secret**. Stand up with your feet slightly apart and squeeze.
- **Ballerina Stance**. Stand with your heels together, toes turned out.
- **Pelvic Thrust**. Lie on your back with your knees bent and open wide, feet flat. Raise your hips and thrust your pelvis forward and back as if you were having sex. Vary the speed at which you thrust.
- **Missionary Squeeze on Top**. Lie on your stomach with your knees bent and slightly open.
- **Ready Steady**. Hold the contraction while you shift positions: keep your legs wide and squeeze as you lie on your back, on your stomach, sideways, then doggy-style.
- **Pelvic Push-up**. Get on your elbows and knees, doggy-style, and squeeze.
- **Pelvic Lunge**: Stand and bring your right leg in front of you as far as you can. Bring your left leg behind you and keep it straight. Both toes should point in the same direction. Bend your right knee slightly and lower your hips. Go low enough to feel a comfortable stretch, but make sure you can maintain your balance. Squeeze, then switch legs.

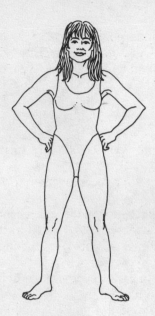

Stand in Secret

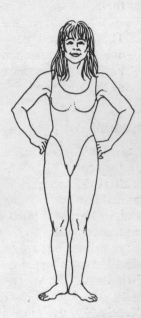

Ballerina Stance

Pelvic Thrust

Missionary on Top

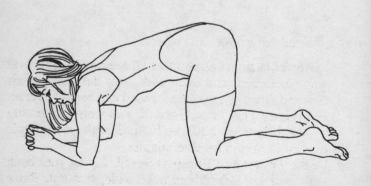

Pelvic Push-up

Pelvic Lunge

Advanced Rhythms

- **Pelvic Thrust and Slow Pump**. Lie on your back with your knees bent and open wide, feet flat. Raise your hips and thrust your pelvis forward and back. Contract and release your muscles as if you were simulating a slow heartbeat. Squeeze in time with your pelvic thrusts. Continue for five minutes.
- **Pelvic Thrust and Pump at Speed**. Lie on your back with your knees bent and open wide, feet flat. Raise your hips and thrust your pelvis forward and back. Speed up your 'slow pump' contractions. Make sure to release each one completely before squeezing again. Continue for five minutes.
- **Pelvic Push-up and Flutter**. Get on your elbows and knees, doggy-style, and squeeze. Flutter the vaginal

muscles by contracting your pelvic floor muscles with few pauses in between. Continue the flutters for as long as you can. Do ten sets of them.

- **Pelvic Lunge and Basic Boogie**. Stand and bring your right leg in front of you as far as you can. Bring your left leg behind you and keep it straight. Both toes should point in the same direction. Bend your right knee slightly and lower your hips. Go low enough to feel a comfortable stretch, but make sure you can maintain your balance. Contract and relax at a moderate speed twenty times. Progress to faster speeds and faster intervals in between. Then switch legs.

- **Pelvic Thrust and Flutter**. Lie on your back with your knees bent and open wide, feet flat. Raise your hips and thrust your pelvis forward and back as if you were having sex. Vary the speed at which you do this. Flutter the vaginal muscles by contracting your pelvic floor muscles with few pauses in between. Continue the flutters for as long as you can. Do ten sets of them.

- **Ballerina and Slow 'n' Easy**. Stand with your heels together, toes turned out. Contract for up to ten seconds, then relax for five seconds and repeat fifty times.

- **Sitting Squeeze with Pelvic Thrust and Slow Pump**. While sitting in a chair with your knees bent and wide apart, move your hips and thrust your pelvis forward and back. Contract and release your muscles as if you were simulating a slow heartbeat. Continue for five minutes.

- **Missionary Squeeze with Pelvic Thrust and Slow Pump**. While lying on your back with your knees bent into your chest and wide apart, move your hips and thrust your pelvis up and down. Contract and release your muscles as if you were simulating a slow heartbeat. Continue for five minutes.

- **Missionary Squeeze on Top with Pelvic Thrust and**

Pump at Speed. While lying on your stomach with your legs wide apart, move your hips and thrust your pelvis up and down. Speed up your 'slow pump' contractions. Be sure to release each one completely before squeezing again. Continue for three minutes.

- **Split Squeeze with Pelvic Thrust and Flutter**. Lie on your back and hold a bent knee into your chest. Keep your other leg straight. Move your pelvis forward and back while you flutter the vaginal muscles by contracting with few pauses in between. Continue each flutter for as long as you can. Do ten sets of them, then switch legs.

- **Side Squeeze with Pelvic Thrust and Pump at Speed**. Lie on one side and extend your top leg out directly in front of your hips. Prop your leg on a pillow to raise it slightly. Keep your bottom leg straight, with your knee slightly bent. Move your hips forward and back as you speed up your 'slow pump' contractions. Make sure you release each one completely before squeezing again. Continue for five minutes, then switch sides.

Remember that exercise is specific. It's only by replicating the movements you do during sex that you'll train your neuromuscular pathway to respond more efficiently during the actual activity. Be creative and include positions from your own personal love-making style to further individualize your routine.

CHAPTER SEVEN

Power Squeezes

Now you're going to go for power and strength. As discussed in Chapter 5, the easiest way to add resistance in order to work your muscles at enough intensity to develop strength, is to use some sort of weight. You probably don't have a set of vaginal dumbbells lying around, so I'll give you a simple way to work hard without using weights. Weighted tools are a good investment, however, and in the Appendix (see page 119) I've listed a few retailers from whom you can obtain the official gynaecological weights or the geisha balls, which are also weighted and a fairly good substitute.

The medical 'Feminacones' are preferable because they come in different sizes so you can increase the resistance as you become stronger. The geisha balls are just one size, but less expensive. Alternatively, if you have a dildo or vibrator you may use that. Even if the weights are quite light, the resistance can challenge your muscles. Make sure whatever you use is hygienic and that you wash and dry it thoroughly before and after use.

First we'll discuss the resistance aids you can use, and then move on to the Power Squeezes themselves.

SEX TOOLS

The Perineometer

This is a measuring device which looks like a big tampon. It is able to detect pressure and has a tube connected to a gauge which gives a reading. When placed in the vagina it provides an indication of how hard the muscles are contracting. It's especially useful for women who are not able adequately to feel the muscles they need to work. This visual device gives instant feedback. Later it is beneficial to measure strength improvements. The disadvantage is that it also may measure intra-abdominal pressure in addition to the pressure resulting from pelvic floor contractions, and so may indicate that you are squeezing the appropriate muscles when you're not. To make sure you are working the right area, do regular checks by doing the finger test. Insert a finger inside your vagina and make sure you feel the pelvic floor muscles squeezing around it.

Vaginal Dumbbells

Studies have shown that training with these produces significantly better pelvic floor muscle strength than exercise without them – in some cases three times as much in the same amount of time. This is not surprising because any muscle group in the body will get stronger more quickly by using weights.

These were devised by a biomedical physicist named Stan Plevnik in 1985 as an alternative method of stimulating the pelvic floor. The weights are metal encased in plastic and shaped like small tampons. Depending upon the manufacturer, they range from 20 to 100g.

Once inserted, the feeling of losing the cone from the vagina is believed to initiate an instinctive response, causing the pelvic floor muscles to contract around the cone to keep it in. In other words, the presence of a foreign object stimulates receptor nerves which result in a distinct feeling in the area. Whereas you normally may have difficulty focusing on where the muscles are, if there is direct stimulus, you are better able to locate them.

There's a lot less concentration needed in comparison to basic squeezing exercises on their own. When the object starts to move, especially as the weight slips out, there is a reflex response which causes the muscles to contract to retain the cone. Again, you'll then be able to identify the contracting sensation and will be more likely to repeat it at will. As you try to keep the weight in by squeezing, you will strengthen the muscle fibres. An increase in strength means an increase in general muscle tone and tightness around the sphincter muscles.

Passive cone weight is the weight of the heaviest cone that can be retained in the vagina for one minute while walking, without voluntarily holding it in; active cone weight is the weight of the heaviest cone that you can voluntarily grip.

Geisha Balls

These are two weighted balls which are attached to each other by a string. They are similar to the weights although technically not as helpful since the weight isn't adjustable. They can be purchased at your nearest sex shop. They can also be used as a substitute for a cuffed catheter, another device commonly used by physiotherapists. This device is placed inside the vagina. As the therapist instructs the patient to squeeze, he or she attempts to pull the item out. You can insert the balls as you would the weights and follow the directions above, or you can create manual resistance by trying to pull them out as you contract your pelvic floor muscles to hold them in.

Others

You can use a dildo, vibrator, or cucumber inside your vagina as other types of resistance tools. (Make sure that anything you use is thoroughly washed and dried before and after use). Insert, sit up straight and try to hold it in.

Then try to walk and hold it in. Lay down and practise your contractions against the device.

Full Range of Motion

When you work your muscles, it's most effective to squeeze them as tight as possible, then to release them completely. Since your emphasis is on the contraction during most of the exercises, focus on totally relaxing between squeezes. This way there will be a noticeable difference between the intense pressure of the contraction, and then the lack of pressure during the squeeze helping you to establish a rhythm. Also you will work the muscle fibres more thoroughly.

It's important to recognize the difference in contracting alone and contracting with something inserted. Because a muscle develops the most strength when it is worked in its full range of motion, although the inserted devices are certainly helpful, they limit your movement. So while inserted tools will help challenge the muscle fibres to work harder, they are only partly worked because of these isometric contractions. Studies have shown that a muscle is strengthened most effectively by combining isometric (limited range of motion) with isotonic (full range of motion) exercises. So continue to do your Sex Squeezes without the tools as well, to work isotonically. That way you can employ full contractions and releases and work the muscle fibres completely.

LEVEL FOUR

Power Squeezes

Perform the exercises described below using one or more of the following methods of resistance:

1. Exercise without additional resistance. When you contract, concentrate on squeezing as tightly as you can each time. Make sure to exhale with the effort. Hold each squeeze. Keep the movement very strong, powerful and controlled. Visualize all the muscle fibres contracting at once.

2. Exercise with weights. Learn how to use the weights first doing basic squeezes before you use them with more complex moves.

Begin with the cone that you can comfortably retain. While standing up, insert the cone into the vagina with the string on the outside so you can pull it out again. You may use lubricant if it is difficult to insert but try to avoid that, because it may become more slippery and harder to hold in. Try to retain the cone for seven minutes a day. Build up to holding in a weight for fifteen minutes, twice daily. You can stand and wait, or get on with housework or other activities to fill the time. The cone will tend to slip out – try to prevent this by contracting your muscles. After you can hold a cone in for this time period for several days, try the next size.

Before increasing the weight, perform the following exercises with your weight inserted.

3. Exercise with other tools (geisha balls, vibrator). Develop a familiarity with the tool use first, as described in the weights section above. Then use the aid while performing the following moves.

- **Power Missionary Squeeze.** Insert your resistance tool or focus on power squeezes. While lying on your back with your knees bent into your chest and wide apart, move your hips and thrust your pelvis up and down. Contract and release your muscles as if you were simulating a slow heartbeat. Continue for five minutes.
- **Power Missionary Squeeze on Top.** Insert your resistance tool or focus on Power Squeezes. While lying on your stomach with your legs wide apart, move your hips and thrust your pelvis up and down. Speed up

your 'slow pump' contractions. Make sure to release each one completely before squeezing again. Continue for three minutes.

- **Power Split Squeeze**. Insert your resistance tool or focus on Power Squeezes. Lie on your back and hold a bent knee into your chest. Keep your other leg straight. Move your pelvis forward and back while you flutter the vaginal muscles by contracting with few pauses in between. Continue each flutter for as long as you can. Do ten sets of them, then switch legs.
- **Power Side Squeeze**. Insert your resistance tool or focus on Power Squeezes. Lie on one side and extend your top leg out directly in front of your hips. Prop your leg on a pillow to raise it slightly. Keep your bottom leg straight, with your knee slightly bent. Move your hips forward and back as you speed up your 'slow pump' contractions. Make sure to release each one completely before squeezing again. Continue for five minutes, then switch sides.
- **Power Pelvic Push-up**. Insert your resistance tool or focus on Power Squeezes. Get on your elbows and knees, doggy-style, and squeeze. Flutter the vaginal muscles by contracting your pelvic floor muscles with few pauses in between. Continue the flutters for as long as you can. Do ten sets of them.
- **Power Pull**. In each of the basic positions (missionary, split, side and the pelvic push-up), insert one of your resistance tools. The weights of geisha balls will work best since they have a string attached. Have you or your partner pull on the string while you simultaneously contract your muscles to resist the object being withdrawn. Once you are stronger, you can even try this with a tampon.

CHAPTER EIGHT

Rhythm Squeezes

Now you're ready to fine tune your movements. There are a few moves to work on alone, then the fun can begin as you practise on your partner! Once you have established a solid base of muscular control, you can progress to working at higher intensities, employing different parts of the pelvic floor muscles. You may want to wait two to four weeks before progressing to this stage, but there will be no harm in doing these exercises sooner. They may be a little more difficult if your overall strength and endurance is not adequate to sustain the more difficult exercises.

Remember how you had to concentrate just to focus on the correct muscles to move? You will need to concentrate again in order to perform more subtle actions.

It may be helpful to imagine the process before, during and after attempts at particularly subtle exercise. This may help you activate desired muscle fibres in isolation. As you visualize, the brain uses similar nerve pathways to those used when actually performing the desired action. Reinforcement by mental training can facilitate the connection. If you think about it, practise it and keep thinking about it, then when you return to it, your performance will be enhanced. This is the theory behind much of the positive visualization that professional athletes do to help them succeed at their sport. Many Olympic medallists imagine themselves performing the perfect run, jump or throw in addition to their daily practice of the skills.

Visualization Exercises

- Pretend that inside your vagina there is a lift. Your job is to move it to the top of your vagina, making three stops on the way. When it reaches the top, hold it before lowering to the ground floor. Pause at each stop. As you do this you should feel as if you are using more and more muscle fibres with each subsequent squeeze. The way down will be harder so go slowly to be as precise in your manoeuvring as possible.
- Imagine your partner's penis is inside and contract your muscles around it. Focus intently and feel yourself pushing against the tip, the middle and down the shaft of his penis. Alternate the sides at which you squeeze.
- With his imagined penis still inside, exhale and contract as strongly as you can to push him out. You can also use your cucumber, dildo or weight on this one. Try to expel it forcefully.
- Imagine sucking the penis in deeper. Notice the difference in the feeling between pushing out and sucking in.
- Imagine squeezing deep within you to grip and envelope the penis tightly. Hold it and imagine that you can squeeze it harder to compress all around it at once. Imagine squeezing so hard that you can milk it.
- Imagine just the outer lips squeezing around the base of the penis. Since this is the area with the most active musculature, develop more strength by contracting as tight as you can. Alternate fast and slow squeezes.

Practise these exercises until you feel that you can distinguish and consciously control different areas of the musculature. These actions are quite subtle so don't get discouraged if all the variations seem to blend into one giant squeeze. The more control and strength you develop, the easier they will become. Even if you feel a little unsure about whether you are able to manipulate the muscles this precisely, you are still exercising them and will continue to see positive results from the practice.

When you feel like you have these moves under control, dim the lights, grab your man and have some fun . . .

CHAPTER NINE

Erotic Exercises

There are endless ways to add variety and pleasure to a dull sex life with your newly toned love muscles. Even doing your daily exercises gets exciting when you're doing them on your partner. After reading these erotic exercises you'll probably want to rush your man to bed to try out some of the new techniques. The fact is, you need to take it slow and easy. The list is so overwhelming that once you're ready to go, you may find you've forgotten everything you've read.

So read all the variations but choose one or two which particularly make you tingle. Think about them. Visualize them. Practise what you can before you get in bed. Then, in the heat of the moment when you're ready to try something new but rushed towards increasing pleasure, rather than revert back to staid old habits you'll have something fresh in your mind. When you've exploited that technique to its potential, possibly even after developing your own personalized variation, then go back to this list and refresh your memory. Include other erotic exercises into your expanding repertoire for exercise ecstasy.

Although you'll both be tempted to act otherwise, remember these moves below are still part of your exercises – erotic exercises, that is. Encourage him to stay put while you fine-tune the muscle action. Take time to visualize what's happening as you do it. Then, if you can't stand it any longer, go ahead and apply some of these techniques to your own love-making style. Or try out some of the ideas in the next chapter so you can travel through the entire phase of human sexual response – from excitement to orgasm and resolution.

LEVEL FIVE

Rhythm Squeezes

Flower Petals

Imagine the delicate lips of your sexy vagina folding and unfolding to caress his penis. Vary the amounts of pressure each petal provides. Make him hold still as you perform this delicate massage. Get his feedback about where he feels the most sensation and notice how that particular squeeze feels to you. Move your hips very slowly up and down the shaft so you can apply varying amounts of pressure to his penis with varying parts of your muscles.

Envelope

Give him a giant bear hug with your pleasure den. With him inside as deep as possible, contract your muscles around his penis. Imagine all the walls, sides, top and bottom coming together for the ultimate in closeness. Hold him tight, tight, and tighter. Hold the squeeze without releasing (remember to breathe regularly).

Climbing the Ladder

Vary your body position during this one as you use the vagina to squeeze your way up and down his penis. Make sure each contraction is very powerful, then release it completely, pause and squeeze again.

Ping Pong

Think sideways as you aim to contract either side of the vaginal walls against his penis. Work your way from the bottom up and then from the top down.

Rocket Launcher

Grip him deep inside you with your muscles. Contract and release rapidly – flutter – then slowly to warm up the engines. Then push him out hard. Repeat the whole process.

Milking

Massage with suction so you milk with your vagina. Tighten and push out, then squeeze in a constricting manner, but not pulling him in. Then push out, constrict, push out, constrict. When you have developed enough strength you should be able to milk him to orgasm.

Quicksand

With every squeeze pull him deeper, deeper inside. Imagine yourself absorbing his penis into your body. Hold it in and flutter your muscles. Then with strong, steady pushes imagine yourself pushing him out of the quicksand. Stop before he ejects completely and squeeze him back in, deeper and deeper.

The Wave

Establish a wave of individual contractions starting with

your anus, progressing to the upper vagina, lower vagina, the urethra. Return from the other direction. This requires precision and concentration so go slowly. Hold each position for a few seconds before proceeding to the next.

The Ripple

Similar to the wave. Once you have travelled through your stopping points, instead of repeating the process backwards, pause and start at the beginning again with your anus. Make the process powerful and quick so it feels as if there are distinct rippling sensations.

Intimate Dance

If you're making love to music replicate the drumbeats of the sound by manipulating the rhythms of your contractions. Try funk, rap, rock and even classical as you move to the mood of the music.

Make sure you exhale and inhale during all of these exercises.

These exercises are certainly erotic, but as long as he is not actively thrusting, you may not experience the tension build-up you need to come. Practise these to excite him while you develop your strength. In the next chapter you get ready for action and use your new strength, endurance and skill to experience orgasmic sexual intercourse.

CHAPTER TEN

Sexstasy

Now you're ready to go for the advanced workout. You're ready to use your skills during sex to help you and your partner experience exercise ecstasy.

As you have noticed with the wide variety of exercises, there are a number of ways to apply your squeezes. During intercourse you can alternate your thrusting and squeezing rhythms, and vary between short strong contractions and long steady holds. The next chapter describes how your partner can strengthen his muscles, too. He can flex his muscles for even more variation and stimulation. Adding this new dimension to intercourse can help you experiment in a whole new way. You no longer need to be the recipient of wham-bam, unfeeling thrusting. You can slow the process down and move with exquisite attention to the union that is taking place.

There are an assortment of different love-making techniques described below. As with the exercises given previously, take it slowly and learn one or two at a time. When you're learning a new skill it's best to do it in the simplest, clearest way possible. Then, when you have the technique mastered, add some variation: a turn here, a twist there, a reversal of limbs – whatever. It's quite important to master the basics before going straight into all the sexual variations because accessory movement is distracting. You can only access more complex coordination processes when the most simple

are firmly established. Learn each technique well and
practise it until grows old. Then expand your repertoire
by adding a few new variations.

Squeezing During Sex Positions

The following positions describe movements you can
do to incorporate your squeezing and thrusting. Some
of the moves require that you work more slowly than
usual; a few have no motion at all. Many Eastern sexual
philosophies suggest that luxuriating in the moments of
joining is more powerful than a quick race to orgasm.
So rather than trying to speed up the pumping process
to achieve your end-result, realize that concentrating this
closeness will enhance your sensation. You will both have
the opportunity to appreciate all the nuances in feeling
that will become obvious when you slow things down.
Most likely, you will both be aroused for longer than
usual, and this too will help increase the intensity of the
orgasms you finally experience. When you've pushed
yourself to the brink and slow moves simply won't do,
then go ahead and thrust, move and screw vigorously.
All the energy you've been building up is going to need
an outlet!

LEVEL SIX

Sexercises

Raise your legs straight above the shoulders of your partner, who is kneeling in front of you and inserting his penis into your vagina. In between his slow thrusts, alternate pressing your thighs together and squeezing him with your Sex Squeezes. This will increase the friction as he moves inside you to produce exquisite sensations for both of you.

With your legs bent at the knee, sit astride, facing your partner on his back. With your vaginal muscles, draw his penis into you and hold it tight for a long time. While he relaxes, imagine pulling it higher inside of you to make it longer and longer and longer . . .

Lie on your back in a split-leg position. With your partner inside, concentrate on squeezing the sides of his penis with the sides of your vaginal wall. Alternate back and forth in a strong pulsating rhythm.

Lay on top of your partner, who is on his back. With him inside, rest on his chest and squeeze his penis and slowly circle your hips five times. Stop, release the squeeze. Then squeeze hard again and rotate your hips in the other direction. Continue this cycle until you are both thoroughly aroused.

With your partner lying on his back, sit on top of him, facing his feet. Place his eager penis inside and then lean back so he can caress your breasts and whisper sweet nothings in your ear! At the base of his penis, hold and squeeze tight. Then, still squeezing, move your pelvis up so your vagina drags as it moves towards the top. Release the squeeze to move to the shaft again and repeat.

In traditional missionary position, with him on top and your legs wrapped around his thighs, squeeze him powerfully as if you are milking or massaging his penis. Alternately squeeze your vaginal muscles and the muscles around the anus, then both together: front, back, both.

With your partner on his side and you on your back, lie perpendicular to each other with your legs elevated resting on his body. Squeeze your muscles in the wave pattern. Establish a wave of individual contractions starting with your anus, progressing to the upper vag, lower vag, then urethra and return from the other direction. This requires precision and concentration so go slowly. Hold each position for a few seconds before proceeding to the next.

Lie on top of him face-down with your head by his feet. Climb a ladder as you vary your body position and use your vagina to squeeze your way up and down his penis. Make sure each contraction is very powerful, then release it completely. Pause and squeeze again.

In traditional doggy-style, try the rocket launcher. Squeeze hard. As he pushes in, you push out. Keep the thrusting as slow and controlled as you can.

Sit astride him on his lap then lean back so your pelvis tilts and puts a bit of upward force on his shaft. Flutter your pelvic floor muscles then release and shift your pelvis up, side, down, side – as if you were aiming for twelve o'clock, three o'clock, six o'clock and nine o'clock. Flutter again and alternate the cycles.

Lie on your back perpendicular to your partner, who is on his side. When he enters, let him thrust. When he thrusts in you squeeze and release as he pulls out.

Sit Indian-style on your partner and thrust towards each other in a controlled rhythm 10 times. Then stop and squeeze powerfully ten times. Continue to alternate as you kiss and cuddle.

Sexstasy Trouble Shooting

- If your knees, back or any other part of your body feels uncomfortable during any of these positions, modify them by straightening a leg, for example, to take the stress off the joint.
- Some positions will be much easier to squeeze in than others. This is due to leg positioning, and is natural.
- Increasing the tension of your love muscles is positive, energy-building tightness. Some tension can be negative or stressful; for instance, when you are holding tension in other parts of your body such as your face, neck and upper back. This kind of tension may reflect anxiety or distress. Or you may be trying too hard. If you cannot fully relax, your orgasm will be weak, or not happen at all. Relax your mind, forget your worries, enjoy. Do not try to force yourself to arousal. Allow it to happen and let the controlled squeezes be a tickling tool for tension, not an energy drainer.

Tightening Tips

- When your squeezing rhythm is quick contractions in fast succession, make sure that you release each contraction fully so there's a noticeable contrast in tightness and pressure.
- Orgasm is achieved by both partners by the slow, steady build-up of tension, friction and pressure on the penis and the clitoris (directly or indirectly). But sometimes the endurance required to get there, the

repetitive pelvic thrusts, continual squeezing, legs held in the same position for extended periods etc. gets tiring. When your muscles fatigue, you have to rest. This momentary lapse in rhythm and tension build-up can delay or even stop the heightening rise to climax. If this happens to you, you can compensate for the halt in pelvic movement by contracting your sex muscles during the breaks. He'll stay hard, you'll stay aroused, and when both pairs of buttocks and thighs have recovered you can resume your thrusts.

- After recovering from a first orgasm, see if you can squeeze him back to erection.
- When he thrusts, try squeezing *before* he enters to tighten the entry. Make sure he keeps his rhythm slow so you can squeeze and release completely each time he has entered you.
- Monitor your breathing and keep it regular. It's very easy when you're still learning how to squeeze hard to hold your breath. Learn to relax your body and breathe easily when you squeeze, you can vary the direction of your breathing: exhale on the squeeze, inhale on the release or inhale on the squeeze and exhale on the release.
- Try squeezing other body parts like your buttocks or thighs, and even varying the pressure of your body squeezing against his.
- Let him enter you soft, and arouse him to delectable hardness with your squeezes.
- If you feel you are on the brink of orgasm, clenching your pelvic floor muscles may help push you to climax.

Use these techniques as a guide, but remember that sex is individual and that your relationship with your partner is individual. Do not feel intimidated if you are not a squeezing virtuoso immediately. Your expertise will come with practise. Rather than stress out, enjoy the training!

Regardless of the level of skill you have attained by now, if you've been practising, you will have undoubtedly experienced wonderful improvements in your lovemaking. Your orgasms should be easier and more fulfilling. Not only has exercise improved your sex life, but your health will have been improved by your orgasms. Orgasms are so successful at releasing tension that they can act as a treatment for backaches, period pains and other ailments. Some studies have even shown that orgasms strengthen the immune system. The word is out. Sexual satisfaction and good health await once you discover the 7-minute sex secret . . .

CHAPTER ELEVEN

Men and their Muscles

Men have pelvic floor muscles, too. If you've ever seen your partner consciously move his penis, those are the same muscles at work. Strong muscles in a man can improve sex for you in many ways. He can move his penis while inside you, to increase pleasurable sensations. If he has a lot of control he can use the contractions to help stop early ejaculation. He can also put his muscles to work to prolong his own ecstasy. Men who have strengthened their muscles may find it easier to achieve and maintain an erection.

Sexologists claim that multiple male orgasms can be achieved with the help of strong pelvic floor muscles. Multiple climaxes known as NEMO or Non-Ejaculatory Male Orgasms, are achieved by the careful balance of stopping at the height of sexual build-up – just before a climax. By controlling how closely he allows himself to come to ejaculation – nearer, nearer, nearer, then backing off before he reaches the point of no return – a man can experience a non-ejaculatory orgasm and keep his erection. Each time he stops he should experience an extreme rush of pleasure. This teasing build-up should make the final ejaculatory episode extremely intense. Theoretically this can go on up to five times, until he's ready to explode.

The skill needed to experience this is learning how to stop ejaculation. Some men can't. Masters and Johnson noted that past a certain point some men were incapable of turning back. Women seem to be able to reach the edge and withdraw much more easily.

How far arousal progresses before a conscious ease-up in tension occurs varies, but most researchers agree that any extended arousal and delayed ejaculation will result in stronger, more intense orgasms. For the man who ejaculates prematurely, learning to control arousal and the build-up of sexual tension will therefore not only be more pleasurable for his partner, but for himself as well.

There are several techniques which can help. Many men are encouraged to be on the bottom during missionary-style intercourse since there appears to be less overall muscle tension in this position, and that can help slow things down. To stop himself from coming a man can simply squeeze the penis. Or he can stop thrusting temporarily. Or he can move his testicles. Or he can clench his pelvic floor muscles intensely just before he feels he is about to come and then totally relax them.

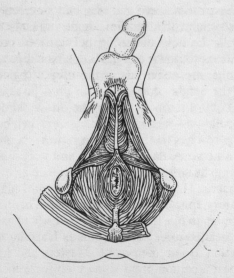

Male Pelvic Floor Muscles

To train his pelvic floor muscles a man can use this simple technique.

- First locate the appropriate muscles. This is most easily done by stopping the urine flow, and many men can consciously wiggle the penis. If they can do that they are activating the right muscles.
- To develop initial strength, your partner can squeeze his muscles and hold for ten to fifteen seconds before contracting again. Aim to build up to doing this 100 times a day to develop endurance.
- Include some squeezing of the muscles in the back portion of the pelvis around the anus. Alternate by tightening the anus, then moving the penis.
- To develop more strength, your partner can rest a small towel on his penis while he does the exercises. Over time he can increase to a heavier towel. Do the strength exercises every other day. Over eight to twelve weeks, your partner can develop enough strength to stop himself from coming just by executing a carefully timed squeeze. With increased control he can manipulate his love tool while he's inside to arouse you and to experience his own multiple orgasms.

CHAPTER TWELVE

7 Minutes to Go

So there you have it: perhaps the first fitness programme *ever* devoted to developing the full potential of your vagina! You have read how at any age pelvic floor muscles can easily become weak. You have seen, and perhaps already experienced, the medical justifications and sexual enticement to strengthen them. There's no doubt that Sex Squeezes are much more entertaining than just about any other workout you might do. They're easy, feel great, and produce quite memorable results. And the accumulated medical evidence shows that you can only benefit from conditioning this area.

As with any other exercise programme, the key is to keep challenging your body. The body's reaction to exercise is a sort of evolutionary response – strength through adversity. Controlled stress stimulates the body to adapt and protect itself. The body grows even stronger and more resilient than it was before so that it can cope with further bouts of stress.

All you need to do is start off with just seven minutes a day of squeezing. If you want to develop advanced strength go on to the more intense exercises. Then, when you've achieved your desired level of conditioning, to maintain your strength just practise your squeezes seven minutes every other day.

For the best possible results, do your Sex Squeezes along with other types of regular exercise (walking, running, aerobics, swimming, and so on.) When you feel good all over, everything overlaps. You'll have more energy, endurance and enthusiasm to enjoy your body. If you are not a regular exerciser, perhaps now that you understand the principles of muscle conditioning and the effects on your health, you will be inspired to add more activity to your daily life.

As life gets busier and conveniences like cars, television, computers, and assorted electrical appliances make us less active, you grow accustomed to not using your body. The less you do, the weaker you get, the harder even small amounts of exertion feel. But even the minimum amount of exercise can have extraordinary effects on your health and psyche. Working out is not just for losing weight. Exercise has become a medical prescription for good mental and physical health. And exercise doesn't have to, and shouldn't be, hard.

In my book, *CURVES – The Body Transformation Strategy*, I show how to pick the type of exercise most suitable for you so you're more likely to stick to it and achieve your goal. As you probably have discovered while reading this book, it's exciting to try the different techniques when they're new and fresh in your mind. But once the initial fervor wears off, it will be easy to miss a few days. Eventually you may forget to do them at all. Like anything good for you, it can be a chore to remember and then practise your exercises. Sticking to the plan may be the most difficult aspect to this regimen. Studies *universally* show that most fitness programmes have a high drop out rate – as many as 50% of those who begin a keep-fit regimen stop within the first six months. But you won't get permanent results if you give up. If you've ever committed wholeheartedly to a new year's resolution and then quit by February, you'll know that the benefits are short-lived unless you develop a habit and integrate it into your lifestyle. A vast amount of research by exercise psychologists has tried to understand what motivates people to continue exercising and what makes them quit. It's easy to go all-out for a very short period. But it's the consistency that makes the difference. Forget miracle results. You'll get more out of doing a little more exercise for the rest of your life rather than 3 weeks non-stop every other January. The more time you spend, naturally the quicker you see results; the results keep you exercising. So to keep your pelvic floor muscles taut and alive, figure out how you can make them a habit.

Sit down and make a list of what you need to do each day and decide in advance when you'll do your exercises. If you truly can't spare the time, think of a way to insert some exercise into your already busy schedule. If you have a favourite TV show, why not do some power squeezes during the commercials? Or if you're stuck in crowded traffic, in jam-packed tubes, or at the end of an endless queue, take those moments to squeeze, squeeze, squeeze! Even better, commit to a whole body fitness programme (even if it's just a short daily stroll through the park) and practise your Sex Squeezes before or after the workout.

When you start doing any type of exercise, it's common to feel as if nothing seems to be happening soon enough. Unfortunately the fad fitness plans and diets which promise miracle makeovers in days have programmed us to expect dramatic changes *fast*. But change takes time. The older you are, the slower physiological adaptions occur. And if you exercise at an easy fitness level, low intensity workouts take longer to give results. Rather than get disappointed, be patient. Be inspired to be even more persistent.

If you're tired, you're probably not going to feel much like doing *anything*. You may have experienced that point when, just after work, you have to decide whether you will work out or just collapse in front of the television and relax. This is usually just mental, not physical fatigue. Since exercise actually boosts your energy levels and raises your circulation, you would probably feel more enthusiastic in the evening and be more apt to stick to your squeezes if you did a light workout – say, a fitness video or cycle around the neighbourhood, than if you just sat on the couch and did nothing once you got home from work.

Getting yourself up off the sofa is absolutely, undeniably the hardest part about exercising. You no doubt had perfectly good intentions to work out and then got sidetracked. You might think, 'I'd rather eat', 'It's cold', or 'I want to read the paper'. Even though Sex Squeezes are much less effort than most exercises – you can still do them while you're on the sofa – you may feel like you simply cannot be bothered to insert a vaginal weight or concentrate enough to do the moves.

That's why the exercises have got to be habitual, like brushing your teeth. Engage yourself in a mental debate when you're feeling unmotivated, think of all the reasons why you should. Remind yourself of what you can achieve. Think sexual ecstasy. Then, before you can analyse it further start squeezing!

I would love to hear about your success with the Sex Squeezes. Send all letters to: Martica, Dept HH1, PO Box 363, London WC2H 9BW, England. I regret that it is not possible to answer reader's letters.

Bibliography

Basmajian MD, John V. and Carlo De Luca PhD. *Muscles Alive – Their Functions Revealed by Electromyography*. 5th Edition. Williams & Wilkins, Baltimore, Maryland USA, 1985.

Bornoff, Nicholas. *Pink Samurai – An Erotic Exploration of Japanese Society*. London: Grafton Books, 1992.

Brauer MD, Alan and Donna. *Extended Sexual Orgasm*. Warner Books, New York, 1984.

Bridges, N., J. Denning, K.S. Olah, and D.J. Farrar. 'A Prospective Trial Comparing Interferential Therapy and Treatment Using Cones in Patients with Symptoms of Stress Incontinence from the Proceeding of the International Continence Society'. *Neurourology and Urodynamics*; Vol. 7, No. 3, 1988.

Chang, Jolan. *The Tao of Love & Sex*. Wildwood House, Hampshire, England, 1986.

Chia, Mantak & Maneewan. *Awaken Healing Light of the Tao*, Healing Tao Books, New York, 1993.

Cutrufelli, Maria Rosa. *Women of Africa – Roots of Oppression*. Zed Press, London, England, 1983.

Darling. PhD, Carol Anderson, J. Kenneth Davidson PhD and Colleen Conway-Welch PhD. 'Female Ejaculation: Perceived Origins, the Grafenberg Spot/Area and Sexual Responsiveness', *Archives of Sexual Behaviour*, Vol. 19, No. 1, 1990.

Delvin, Dr David. *Love Play*. London: Ebury Press, 1994.

Eisenberg, Arlene, Heidi E. Murkoff & Sandee E. Hathaway. *What to Expect when You're Expecting*. London: Simon & Schuster, 1991.

Fleck, Steven J. and William J. Kraemer. *Designing Resistance Training Programs*. Human Kinetics Books, 1987.

Gray, Henry. *Gray's Anatomy*. New York: Bounty Books, 1977.

Grayber B, and Kelin Grayber, *Female Orgasm*, Journal of Clinical Psychiatry, 1979, p.318–35.

Hay, Margaret Jean and Sharon Stichter. *African Women South of the Sahara*. Longman, 1984.

Heiman, Julia R. and Joseph LoPiccolo. *Becoming Orgasmic – A Sexual and Personal Growth Programme for Women*. London: Piatkus, 1988.

Hite, Shere. *The Hite Report*. London: Pandora, 1976.

Hooper, Anne. *Kama Sutra*, London: Dorling Kindersley, 1994.

Jackson, Michelle. 'Women's Health'. *Ultrafit Magazine*. Vol. 4, No. 6, 1994.

Janus PhD, Samuel, and Cynthia Janus MD. *The Janus Report on Sexual Behaviour*. John Wiley & Sons, Inc., 1993.

Jonasson, Aino, Bertil Larsson and Helmut Pschera. 'Testing and Training of the Pelvic Floor Muscles After Childbirth'. *Acta Obstetrics Gynaecology Scandinavia*. 68: 301–304, 1989.

Jones III MD, Howard, Anne Colsten Wentz MD, Connie Burteh MD. *Novak's Textbook of Gynaecology*. 11th Edition, William St Wikins, Baltimore, 1988.

Kakar, Sudhir. *Intimate Relations – Exploring Indian Sexuality*. Chicago: The University of Chicago Press, 1989.

The Kama Sutra of Vatsyayana. Translated by Sir Richard Burton and F.F. Arbuthnot. London: Grafton Press, 1963.

Kaplan, Helen Singer MD, PhD. *The New Sex Therapy*, London: Bailliere Tindall, 1974.

Kapit, Wynn, and Lawrence M. Elson. *The Anatomy Coloring Book*. New York: Harper & Row Publishers, 1977.

Kegel MD, A.H. 'Progressive Resistance Exercise in the Functional Restoration of the Perineal Muscle'. *American Journal of Obstetrics & Gynaecology: 56: 238–248, 1948.*

Kegel MD, Arnold H. 'Sexual Functions of the Pubococcygeus Muscle', *Western Journal of Surgery for Obstetrics and Gynaecology*, Oct. 1952, p.521–24.

Kegel MD, Arnold. 'The Physiologic Treatment of Poor Tone and Function of the Genital Muscles and of Urinary Stress Incontinence', *Western Journal of Surgery for Obstetrics and Gynaecology*, Nov. 1949, p.527–33.

Laycock, J. 'Graded Exercises for the Pelvic Floor Muscles in the Treatment of Urinary Incontinence', *Physiotherapy Journal*, Vol. 73, 1987, p.371–373.

Mackay, Eric, N. Beischer, R. Pepperall, C. Woo. *Illustrated Textbook of Gynaecology*. 2nd Edition, W.B. Saunders, Harcourt Brace Jovanovich, New York, 1992.

Masters MD, William H. interview. 12 December, 1994.

Masters, William H. and Virginia E. Johnson. *Human Sexual Response*. Boston: Little. Brown and Company, 1966.

Masters, William H. and Virginia E. Johnson. *Human Sexual Inadequacy*. London: J & A Churchill Ltd, 1970.

Masters MD, William H. 'The Sexual Response Cycle of the Human Female'. *Western Journal of Surgery for Obstetrics and Gynaecology*, Jan.-Feb. 1960, p.57–72.

Masters MD, William H, Virginia E. Johnson DSc, Robert C Kolodny MD. *Heterosexuality*. London: Thorsons, 1994.

McArdle, William D, Frank Kath and Victor Katch, *Exercise Physiology*, Leak & Febiger, Philadelphia, 1986.

Mishell Jr. Daniel, and Paul Brenner. *Management of Common Problems in Obstetrics & Gynaecology*, 3rd Edition. Blackwell Scientific Publications, 1994.

Mumford, Dr John. *A Chakra & Kundalini Workbook – Psycho-Spiritual Techniques for Health, Rejuvenation, Psychic Powers & Spiritual Realization*. Llewellyn Publications, St Paul, Minnesota USA, 1994.

Olah, Karl S. 'Sexual Dysfuntion Associated with Vaginal Laxity'. *The Journal of Sexual Health*. March 1992.

Olah, MB CHB, Karl S. Nina Bridges MCSP, Jan Denning SRN and David Farrar MS FRCS. 'The conservative management of patients with symptoms of stress incontinence: A randomized, prospective study comparing weighted vaginal cones and interferential therapy'. *American Journal of Obstetrics and Gynaecology* 1990: 162: 87–92.

Parker, Richard G. *Bodies. Pleasures and Passions* –

Sexual Culture in Contemporary Brazil. Boston: Beacon Press 1991.

Peattie, A.B., S. Plevnik, S.L. Stanton. 'Vaginal Cones: A Conservative Method of Treating Genuine Stress Incontinence'. *British Journal of Obstetrics and Gynaecology*, October 1988. 95: 1049–1053.

Peattie, A.B. and S. Plevnik. 'Cones versus Physiotherapy as Conservative Management of Genuine Stress Incontinence from the Proceeding of the International Continence Society'. *Neurourology and Urodynamics*: Vol. 7. No.3. 1988.

Penney, Alexandra. *How To Make Love to a Man (Safely).* London: Vermilion, 1993.

The Perfumed Garden of the Shaykh Netzawi – A Comprehensive Treatise on Love. Translated by Sir Richard Burton. London: Harper Collins Publishers, 1993.

Ramsdale, David and Ellen. *Sexual Energy Ecstasy, A Practical Guide to Lovemaking Secrets of the East and West.* Bantam Books, New York, 1993.

Rawson, Philip. *The Art of Tantra*, London: Thames and Hudson, 1993.

Rawson, Philip. *The Art of Tantra*. Thames and Hudson, London, 1993.

Ridley, Ed by CM. *The Vulva.* Churchill Livingstone, 1988

St Clare, Olivia. *203 Ways to Drive a Man Wild in Bed.* Doubleday, 1993.

Swift, Rachel. *Women's Pleasure or How to have an orgasm as often as you want.* Pan Books, 1993.

Truong, Thanh-dam. *Sex, Money and Morality – prostitution and tourism in south-east asia.* Zed Books Ltd, 1990.

Westcott PhD, Wayne. *Strength Fitness – Physiological Principles and Training Techniques.* Brown & Benchmark, 4th Edition, 1995.

Westcott PhD, Wayne. interview.

Osborne MD, John. interview.

Zaviacic, Milan and Beverly Whipple. Update on the Female Prostate and the Phenomenon of Female Ejaculation, *The Journal of Sex Research*, Vol 30, No 2: 148–151, May 1993.

Appendix

Vaginal Weights

FeminaCones: weighted inserts come in a range of sizes so that as you increase pelvic floor strength, you can increase the resistance for further improvement.
Colgate Medical
1 Fair Acres Estate
Dedworth Road
Windsor
Berks SL4 4LE
01753 860 378

Geisha balls: weighted spheres which can be used instead of the vaginal weights.

Duo Balls from Ann Summers
2 Godstone Road
Whyteleafe
Surrey CR3 OEA
0181 660 0102

Also from Aphrodite
PO Box 47
M21 3EJ

AquaFlex vaginal cones are available from:
DePuy Healthcare
Millshaw House
Manor Mill Lane
Leeds LS11 8LQ
0800 614 086

Pelvic Floor Exerciser (PFX)

The PFX is a vaginal probe which, when squeezed by the pelvic floor muscles, displaces air which travels to a pressure sensor. The signal from this sensor shows the strength and duration of the squeeze. This feedback helps record improvements in strength from doing the Sex Squeezes.

In the UK:

Neen Health Care
Old Pharmacy Yard
Church Street
East Dereham
Norfolk NR19 1DJ
Tel: 01362 698960

In Australia:

Cardio Design Pty Ltd
PO Box 778
Castle Hill
NSW 2154
Australia
Tel: 010 612 899 7463

Order Martica's other books and videos!

BOOKS:

CURVES The Body Transformation Strategy

Curves shows you *exactly* how to achieve your personal goal: decrease fat, resculpt your physique, increase your energy, improve your health or just relax and experience peace through movement. Learn more about weight loss, injury, fat, muscle, motivation, exercise myths and more! Discover the perfect exercise plan for you, then learn how to stick to it so you see results. Available from Hodder & Stoughton, 338 Euston Road, London, NW1 3BH. Price £9.99.

Secrets of an Aerobics Instructor

If you are interested in becoming a fitness teacher, this book gives you insights on how to develop, analyse and improve your instructing skills and techniques.

How To Be A Personal Tutor

If you are interested in entering the lucrative field of personal fitness training, use this manual to start up.

VIDEOS:

The 7 Minute SEX Secret Total Body Workout

An invigorating and stimulating workout to get your whole body ready for great sex! Increase your stamina in an energy-increasing aerobics routine. Develop perfect pelvic muscle control and firm up your sex muscles with Sex Squeezes!

CURVES – The Body Transformation Workout

This multi-part video offers you several different workout combinations to keep the variety in your fitness routine. Burn fat, increase energy-levels, strengthen your hips, thighs, buttocks, abdominals and upper body. Easy to follow.

Thighs, tums & bums

Burn fat calories by CardioSculpting – low impact aerobics with tough leg work for your hips and thighs. Also includes a flattening abdominal section. Simple moves and clear explanations make this workout good for men and beginners as well as experienced exercisers. Given top reviews by leading magazines and papers.

Make cheque/po payable to Mind & Muscle

Send order to PO Box 363, Dept HH, London WC2H 9BW

24 HOUR CREDIT CARD HOTLINE: 0171 240 9861

Name

Address

Postcode:

Tel:

Please send _____ copies of *CURVES* the video for £12.99 each   £

Please send _____ copies of 7 Minute SEX Secret Total Body Workout Video – £12.99   £

Please send _____ copies of *Thighs, tums & bums* low impact video – £12.99   £

Please send _____ copies of *Secrets* for just £19.99 each   £

Please send _____ copies of *Personal Trainer* for £14.99 each   £

All prices include p + p in the UK;
Countries outside of the UK add £5.00 per item   £

Credit cards accepted: VISA/MC/Access/Eurocard/JCB/AMEX   **Total Amount**   £
    Number: _ _ _ _ _ _ _ _ _ _ _ _ _ _ _ _

    Expiry: _ _ /_ _

Signature